PORTRAIT OF AMERICA

BY DIEGO RIVERA

WITH AN EXPLANATORY TEXT BY BERTRAM D. WOLFE. NEW YORK: COVICI · FRIEDE, PUBLISHERS

MANUFACTURED IN THE UNITED STATES OF AMERICA
BY J. J. LITTLE AND IVES COMPANY, NEW YORK

REPRODUCTIONS BY THE KNUDSEN PROCESS

Designed by Robert Josephy

FIRST PRINTING APRIL 1934

SECOND PRINTING APRIL 1937

CONTENTS

ACKNOWLEDGMENTS

THANKS are due the following for the use of material in making the reproductions in this book: Carl Zigrosser and the Weyhe Gallery, for the photographs of "The Drillers," "Frozen Assets," and the San Francisco Stock Exchange mural, and for the lithograph self-portrait of Diego Rivera reproduced on the jacket; Gabriel Moulin, for the photograph of the San Francisco School of Fine Arts mural; Lucienne Bloch, for her photographs of the Rockefeller Center mural; S. Lucas, for the photographs of the Detroit Museum murals; Peter Juley, for the photographs of the New Workers' School murals; and Walker Evans, for his photographs of many details from the same series.

INTRODUCTION

INTRODUCTION *BY DIEGO RIVERA*

THE social development of our time is a continuous, accelerated march towards collectivization, and for this reason the necessity for mural painting, the character of which is essentially collective, becomes ever more urgent. In reality, the advanced, modern architecture of today has provided fresco painting as never before with its *raison d'être*. The unequalled trinity of modern construction, steel, glass, and concrete, would in itself be the best reason for the birth of fresco in our day, if fresco were not already as ancient as the first buildings in which man employed mortars on a base of lime or cement for his architectural efforts. Fresco is the only form of painting which finds its true place as readily in the light, soaring constructions of steel, concrete, and glass which we erect today as on the gigantic heavy walls of earlier architecture.

Tomorrow, architecture, the mother of all the plastic arts, will be rationalized, will slough off the leprous scales of its traditional ornamentation and vomit the useless trumperies and horrible gingerbread adornments from its walls, in order to substitute for these a rationalized dwelling whose bright walls are splendidly illuminated by great spaces of glass and light—a dwelling suitable to the cerebral functioning of civilized man who has conquered himself by means of the machines he has built and has thrown off the diseases of mystic ideologies. Only so can true mural painting grow in splendor and importance and play its part in helping mankind to traverse the road that leads to the classless society of the future.

But today as well, mural painting must help in man's struggle to become a human being, and for that purpose it must live wherever it can; no place is bad for it, so long as it is there permitted to fulfill its primary functions of nutrition and enlightenment.

It was with these ideas already partially formulated that I returned from France to Mexico in 1921 in search of walls to paint. I had never painted in fresco up to this time, and I learned the technique of my craft from masons and housepainters, for these journeymen painters of Mexico have kept alive the art of fresco painting since those remote times when the entire surface and the sculptures of ancient Indian architecture were covered, in fresco, with beautiful colors.

In Mexico, I was forced to use what walls I could find, almost invariably old and covered with the ravages of nitrate, and enclosed in a lamentable architecture; or else in newly constructed buildings of atrocious style and taste, built, which is worse, with materials salvaged from the demolition of older structures already contaminated with the leprosy of saltpetre, as in the Secretariat of Public Education.

Between the nitrate and the "decent" people of Mexico, my frescoes were often damaged and partially destroyed, to the great satisfaction of the bourgeoisie and especially the Spanish sections thereof, religious bigots and enslavers of men, as well as to the dissimulated hypocritical rejoicing of the thieving and corrupt counter-revolutionary official bureaucracy, social elements who were also enraged by the form and, above all, by the content of my Mexican frescoes.

On the other hand, the peasants and workers of Mexico liked and enjoyed my frescoes, an experience which authorizes me to declare that for them my work was of value—and that is all that interests me.

Mexico is much more an agricultural than an industrial country, and one, moreover, whose agriculture, based on a poor, primitive, and defective soil, must still struggle painfully, under the yoke of foreign imperialism and of the brutal repression of the national capitalism which daily assassinates peasants throughout the entire country, to emerge from semi-feudalism and colonial slavery. Consequently, the painting I did in Mexico had to conform to these circumstances and was necessarily of a predominantly peasant character.

Thus, the larger experiment in mural painting, of which all my work since 1921 has been a part, could not be completely realized in Mexico. Its early stages had produced very satisfactory results, but it was urgently necessary for me to continue it in a highly industrialized country, under conditions impossible to find in Mexico. Only by testing the action and reaction between my painting and great masses of industrial workers could I take the next step towards my central objective—that of learning to produce painting for the working masses of the city and country.

Now, Mexican economy depends on the North-American bourgeoisie, and the United States, a country of the same soil as Mexico, part of the same continent, is the land in which industrialization has reached a maximum degree of development, along with that great concentration of capital which culminates in imperialism. It was thus the most propitious place in which to continue my work. For years I had been waiting for the first opportunity offered me to enter the United States with my work and there make the attempt to complete the experiment which occupied my whole attention.

When Mr. Ralph Stackpoole, of San Francisco, a sculptor whom I had known well in Paris, came to Mexico, I spoke to him of my plans. Mr. Stackpoole very generously interested himself in my work and did his utmost, after his return to San Francisco, to interest others there, with such success that Mr. William Lewis Gerstle, President of the Society of Fine Arts of San Francisco, donated the sum of $1,500 for a fresco to be painted by me if I should ever go there.

I was unable immediately to avail myself of this offer because I had been invited by the Soviet Commissariat of Education to attend the tenth anniversary celebration of the October Revolution in Moscow. Not until 1930, some time after my return to Mexico from Russia, was I at last free to go to San Francisco. Ralph Stackpoole had not stopped his efforts on my behalf, and during the time that had elapsed he had succeeded in interesting others of his friends in a second proposal. The architect, Timothy Pflueger, who had just finished constructing the new building of the San Francisco Stock Exchange, suggested that I paint a mural in the interior staircase of the building's Luncheon Club, where Stackpoole, Clifford Wight, and other artists had worked together on the decorative scheme.

California was for me the ideal intermediate step between Mexico and the United States. Although it is also more agricultural than industrial, its agriculture is highly advanced and mechanized; its mining districts are very like the part of Mexico where I was born, even though the primitive mining technique of my boyhood days bore little enough relation to the methods in use here; and the state as a whole is a rich land intimately bound up with the remains of its earlier Mexican character, forming a transition stage between the industrial East and primitive, backward Mexico; a region whose mountains and deserts are the connecting link between the strong, bitter, rugged landscape of Mexico and the flat plains and lake-dotted rolling hills of the Middle West, North, and East, the cradle of America's industrialization.

My fresco in the Stock Exchange Luncheon Club objectifies the productive resources of California and typifies its workers—the agriculturist and horticulturist, expressed by the figure of Luther Burbank; the ranchers, the miners and gold prospectors, represented by Marshall, the discoverer who gave the signal for the Gold Rush; the mechanic, man of the mines and tractors and steamships and oil-wells. In the midst of these, I placed the young worker-student, holding in his hand the model of an airplane. California itself is symbolized by a large female figure—a woman of tanned skin and opulent curves modeled after the rolling hills of the landscape, with one hand opening the sub-soil to the labor of the miners, and with the other offering the ripe fruits of the earth.

The painter's intention, of course, must not lie outside the function of the place in which his painting has its being, else his work will be lacking in both objective and subjective correctness and truth. In this mural in a luncheon club, I painted the fruits of the earth which enrich and nourish because of the productive labor of workers and farmers. I painted no mortgage-holding bankers, or industrial overlords, or parasitic exploiters—only the modern workers and discoverers, as well as the pioneers and those brave adventurous guides of the prairie schooners which brought the bloodthirsty hordes across the lands defended by the free Indians, there to become despoiling adventurers, persecutors of Mexicans, populators of the land of gold; all those barbarous settlers and entrepreneurs who were as necessary as the fatal crimes they committed in the process of transforming this new land by industrialization into something that would, as Marx foretold in a brilliant prophecy, convert the Atlantic Ocean into an inland sea and make the Pacific the new ocean of world commerce.

I was reproached by many people for not having included a portrait of Tom Mooney in the Luncheon Club mural, and there might be some justification for their criticism if one did not also take into account the place in which I was painting. But I believe implicitly that a work of art is true only if its function is realized in harmony with the building or room for which it has been created, and I cannot bring myself to believe that the place for an image of Tom Mooney, victim of a bourgeois frame-up and martyr in the social war, is an exclusive restaurant dedicated to the sole use of its stockbroker members. What I painted for them there was designed to show them that what they eat and what enriches them are the products of the toil of workers and not of financial speculation—the natural beauty of California, fertilized by the vigor of workers, farmers, and scientists.

Later, when at Rockefeller Center in New York I painted the naked and objective truth about the essential factors of social strife, and included a portrait of Lenin, I did so because Rockefeller Center is a group of public buildings open to all the inhabitants of the city and containing theaters, lecture halls, offices, radio and television studios, laboratories, and even a subway station! There I could only paint that which corresponded to and was significant for the entire mass of producing citizens; for the buildings which today have been erected out of the capitalist drive for profits, will tomorrow, because of their public functional utility, be delivered over into the hands of the workers. Tomorrow there will be no stock exchanges or brokers or frescoes in their luncheon clubs, and if, by some chance, the victorious working class should preserve my Stock Exchange fresco, it will be only for whatever historical value it may possess; while the Rockefeller Center mural would have been just as relevant after the establishment of the new social order as it was when I painted it, for then, as now, radio stations, television, theaters, great buildings, and subways will be just as necessary to the collectivity of man.

The fresco I painted in the San Francisco School of Fine Arts seems to me to express exactly the objective situation which produced it and to contain, technically, all the possibilities of mural painting; and, since it was executed in a technical school of the plastic arts, these, naturally, had to be its first functions.

The wall is subdivided into cells by the scaffold, which is the necessary pre-construction for all buildings. The scaffold is not only visible, it constitutes the very frame of the work and indicates the structural simplicity and plastic honesty of the composition. The various cells which it establishes contain all the elements of architectural construction; in the center and base, are the machine, the engineer, the architect, and the donor; on either side, the raw materials, and the trained workers who construct and operate the machine and those who calculate and trace the plans of construction; above these draftsmen are the metal workers who are raising the steel skeleton of the building, and opposite them, above the mechanics and iron forgers, the sculptors are giving living form to the stone with chisels driven by the power of air compressed by the machine; above the sculptors, the ventilators, those beautiful functional sculptures created by industrial necessity, renew the air of the factory; in the center, on the planks of the scaffold, are the painters and masons working on a fresco which shows the gigantic figure of a worker grasping the power control of the machine with his right hand and with his left the lever which regulates its speed. His head completes the composition at its highest point, and his gaze is fixed firmly forward. . . .

These two frescoes completed my work in California, and, as I have suggested, served me as a sort of transition from Mexico and as an introduction to the United States. From there I looked forward, to undertake the following year the beginning of my "portrait" of America.

While I was still in California, I was presented to Dr. William Valentiner, Director of the Detroit Museum of Art. I confided to him my project of interpretation of the industrial life of the United States and the possibilities I saw in the development of a series of murals based on a given industry, making plastic the beautiful, continually ascending rhythm moving from the extraction of the raw material, product of nature, to the final elaboration of the finished article, the product and expression of human intelligence, will, and action; and, surrounding and interpreting this rhythm, the expression in plastic values of the social implications of the life of the producers.

Dr. Valentiner was greatly interested in my plans, and several months later, before I had left California, I received a concrete proposal from him to paint a series of murals in the Detroit Museum on the industrial life of the city. The cost of the work was to be borne by the President of the Detroit Commission of Art, Mr. Edsel B. Ford.

The industries of Detroit—metallurgy, industrial and biological chemistry, and the mechanics of the automobile—were precisely those which most suited my taste as subjects for painting, and I accepted the proposal with the greatest enthusiasm. Unfortunately, I was unable to go at once, as I had to return to Mexico where I was being called to continue work on the frescoes I had already begun on the central staircase of the National Palace. While I was there, another prospective commitment became definite. Some time before, the Directors of the Museum of Modern Art in New York, Messrs. Jere Abbott and Alfred Barr, whom I had met in Moscow in 1928, had asked me to give a retrospective one-man show of my work in New York. I now accepted this invitation as well, and came to New York in the Fall of 1931.

Together with my drawings and oils, the Modern Museum wished to exhibit several examples of my murals, and in spite of the fact that I had never considered mural painting to be anything but a painting executed in a determined architectural place and space, I was nevertheless interested by this idea as an opportunity to show the New York public several movable panels painted in fresco—merely, of course, as a sample, to show technical methods of work. The themes I chose were several free replicas of some of my Mexican frescoes, and three whose subjects were the result of observations in New York; a composition built around the work in an electric power plant; a group of workers with pneumatic drills (page 37); and a cross-section of the city, which the newspapers baptized "Frozen Assets" (page 39).

From New York I went to Detroit, and in that city I found waiting for me and ready to hand marvelous plastic material which years and years of work could not exhaust. I should have liked to remain there eight or ten years at least, to manipulate, digest, understand, and express the material in a planned and carefully thought out scheme of work. Unluckily, I had but one year in Detroit, and during that year I did as much as I could and lived what was perhaps the best and most fruitful period of my life. I painted twenty-seven panels of various sizes on the walls of the covered central courtyard of the Detroit Museum, and at the same time, stored up within myself sufficient material for many years of future work. The full direct contact, which I was experiencing at last, with the massed industrial proletariat and with its methods of production, and the intensive study of the workers from the plastic point of view, made that single year worth at least ten in my development as an artist and in the clarification of my social outlook and mentality.

I have always maintained that art in America, if some day it can be said to have come into being, will be the product of a fusion between the marvelous indigenous art which derives from the immemorial depths of time in the center and south of the continent (Mexico, Central America, Bolivia, and Peru), and that of the industrial worker of the north. The dynamic productive sculptures which are the mechanical masterpieces of the factories, are active works of art, the result of the genius of the industrial country developed in the historico-social period which canalized the plastic genius of the superior and gifted individual within the broad stream of the workers for the creation of industrial mechanical art. Bridges, dams, factories, locomotives, ships, industrial machinery, scientific instruments, automobiles, and airplanes are all examples, and merely a few of them chosen at random, of this new collective art.

A machine is an assemblage of indispensable materials, and its forms and essential proportions are planned in immediate and direct relation to its function; that is to say, a machine that lives, and performs the functions for which it was intended, must have been constructed under inevitably harmonic conditions. Do not painting, sculpture, and architecture require the same harmony and functional utility to be considered as really living, dynamic, and socially enlightening?

When my Detroit frescoes were completed, I obtained indirect proof of their value and of the efficiency of the experiment I had carried out and the correctness of the line I had followed. If my work has a purpose, it may be summed up as being to make the greatest contribution of which I am capable to the esthetic nourishment of the working class, in the form of clarifying expression of the things that class must understand in its struggle for a classless society. All the social elements of Detroit which represent the forces of resistance against that purpose reacted violently, almost hysterically, against my frescoes. Elegant clubwomen and preachers employed every available means, from society gossip and slander to the anathema of Heaven, to undo the work I had accomplished, and even raised a cry for the whitewashing of my paintings on the ground of their "un-Americanism," the un-Americanism of the Detroit factories and workers! Is this not a marvelous example of the esthetic-nationalistic logic of the bourgeoisie?

These same sectors of the bourgeoisie, and in particular all the representatives of the various religious orders and faiths, charged that my worked showed me to be an atheist, a materialist, and a bolshevik, and that I had painted absolutely nothing "spiritual." As a matter of fact, my Detroit frescoes, which are nothing but a simple plastic expression of the subjective and objective truth of the time and place in which I was working, contain not the slightest tinge of demagogy, nor are they paintings of agitation. But the opinion of the "nice" people of Detroit was not unexpected, and I could hardly ask the class enemies of the proletariat for a better confirmation of the essential rightness of my work.

But the direct uncontestable proof of the validity of my experiment was furnished by the thousands of industrial workers, who formed a united front to defend my murals in whatever fashion it might be necessary. The factory workers, the youth, the school boys, came day after day by the hundreds to see the frescoes; their enthusiasm was for me the clearest demonstration of the worth of the decade of experimentation in art for the masses which I was just completing.

In the last few months of my work in Detroit, I received a definite offer to paint three panels in the lobby of the RCA Building in Rockefeller Center. Matisse and Picasso, I was informed, were to be offered the two lateral corridors in which each was to paint five panels. I was very doubtful that these two painters would accept, and said so to the architect of the building who was negotiating with me; nevertheless, the possible company of these painters (which was certainly good company), and above all the large, well-proportioned, and well-lighted wall that was offered me, decided me to accept. Even the theme was not bad, although it had been worded in very pretentious terms by the general staff of the management: "Man at the Crossroads Looking with Uncertainty but with Hope and High Vision to the Choosing of a Course Leading to a New and Better Future."

From the very beginning, I explained to the architects, as well as to the owners and management of the building, my interpretation of the theme—for a man of my opinions, the only possible interpretation. The crossed roads were the individualist, capitalist order, on the one hand, and the collectivist, socialist order, on the other; and Man, the Producer, in his triple personality of worker, farmer, and soldier, stood at their intersection. Thus, my composition would synthesize, contrasting them by means of their most typical realities, the two opposed concepts; and Man would be represented, naturally, as the skilled worker, the worker who is also man of science, the classless man, controlling by means of the machine which is the child of scientific knowledge, the vital productive energy in order to canalize it from its various natural functions into the broad stream of fundamental human necessity: that is to say, production in the hands of the producer and not of the exploiter.

I had also to take into account the fact that the wall offered me was well situated in an open and public site and that it was of the utmost importance to utilize it well; for, no matter what the outcome of the events that the painting must surely have produced, they would in any case constitute a most valuable test, as the mural would indubitably, if correctly done, focus international interest on its social significance.

As I had expected, the painters first proposed refused the commission. Matisse objected that neither the building nor the size of the wall was suited to his intimate style; while Picasso would not even receive Raymond Hood, the architect, nor Mr. Todd, of the contractors, to discuss the project with them. Since they were unable to secure the work of these two good painters, the management thereupon engaged José María Sert and Frank Brangwyn.

But this put another face on the matter for me, and my first reaction, as a painter, was naturally to refuse the commission. Moreover, Mr. Todd was insisting at all cost that the painting must be a canvas mural of the usual "expensive wallpaper" type, and with good reason, for such murals avoid difficulties, distract no one from the weighty affairs of business, and are so "distinguished" that no one sees them; thus bourgeois digestions are not upset, nor is the risk run of arousing the unrest of exploited employes.

Two members of the owners' family, however, were interested—or so they assured me—in having at least one true mural in the building, and they insisted that I accept the commission. They supported my opinion that the painting be done in fresco and in colors, so as to "center" the series of murals, as well as to emphasize the point of the axis of the group of buildings, something which was obviously necessary and finally admitted even by the architects. Only Mr. Todd still held out for black and white, and on the day that the final meeting was held to authorize the use of fresco and of color, he preferred to go rabbit-hunting rather than take part in a decision which he considered a violation of all those principles of esthetics, ethics, religion, and capitalist politics which he held sacred.

The Rockefeller Center architects had always wanted to use black and white in the decorations. One of them, perhaps the most modern of them all, and, as far as painting was concerned, with the most cultivated taste, had mentioned to me that his personal preference was for canvas murals which would be "something like Chinese painting." I have no idea why he conceived the notion of going to painters who have a definite personality and a style of their own to produce anything of that sort. As for the other architects of the project, the one among them who enjoyed the greatest authority and renown told me frankly, on a number of occasions, that he understood nothing of painting, something which seemed to me undeniable. Moreover, subsequent events have demonstrated that, like the majority of their American colleagues turned out by the Paris École de Beaux Arts, they can only tolerate as mural painting those nauseating productions of the infra-academic painters deriving from the same school, or of the stepsons of that famous establishment.

A small amount of reflection will, I think, enable anyone to realize that the only things these architects really like to paste on the walls of their buildings are canvas enlargements of the vulgarest kind of illustration from the popular magazines, done in oils, and as slick, smooth, and shiny as the patent leather pumps which they wear to their evening parties. (Historical note: Mr. Todd, in the contracts drawn up under his orders, insisted on inserting the express condition that the murals done in oils must be given at least five coats of varnish!)

Needless to say, the problem, for me, was totally different. It was the problem of painting a fresco that would be useful to the working people of New York, since the producers have enriched the financiers who "own" the building; and, in all justice, it is to the working people of the city and of the world that Rockefeller Center really belongs. Thus, I considered that the only correct painting to be made in the building must be an exact and concrete expression of the situation of society under capitalism at the present time, and an indication of the road that man must follow in order to liquidate hunger, oppression, disorder, and war. Such a painting would continue to have esthetic and social value—and still greater historical value—when the building eventually passed from the hands of its temporary capitalist owners into those of the free commonwealth of all society.

The owners of the building were perfectly familiar with my personality as artist and man and with my ideas and revolutionary history. There was absolutely nothing that might have led them to expect from me anything but my honest opinions honestly expressed. Certainly I gave them no reason to expect a capitulation. Moreover, I carried my care in dealing with them to the point of submitting a written outline (after having prepared the sketch which contained all the elements of the final composition) in detailed explanation of the esthetic and ideological intentions that the painting would express. There was not in advance, nor could there have been, the slightest doubt as to what I proposed to paint and how I proposed to paint it.

In the actual work, which I tried to carry out to the best of my ability and to make superior to anything I had done before, I was assisted with the generous collaboration of distinguished scientists, engineers, biologists, inventors, and discoverers, one of them an important research worker in a well-known scientific institution supported by the owners of Rockefeller Center. Doctor and biologist of international reputation, he carried his generosity to the extent not only of lending me his biological skill and knowledge to be made plastic on the wall, but of working at my side night after night, sometimes until three o'clock in the morning, so that the material he supplied me might possess its correct social and esthetic function in the finished painting. Talented young artists, some of them at the beginning of a brilliant career, sacrificed their time and gifts in order to become my assistants. And the workmen engaged in the construction of the still unfinished building took such an interest in the progress of the fresco that they would arrive an hour before their day's work began in order to watch us, much to the annoyance of the foremen and private guards of the owners, whose job it was to police them.

Large numbers of the outside public, as well as many qualified specialists, took a lively interest in the work. I think it may be said that all the positive social forces were for it, and, naturally, only the negative forces against it. There was nothing grandiloquent or demagogic in the painting, nothing that did not correspond accurately to the reality of the existing social situation. It was a work of art made to function in society, and it is no self-flattery to believe that its purpose would have been fulfilled. Had its functioning been less efficient, its interpretation of the given theme less penetrating and accurate, the bourgeoisie would not have proceeded against it with all the force and power at their command and, finally, destroyed it.

The attack was at first veiled, and couched in the courteous language of diplomacy. But when the painter failed to give ground before the conciliatory offers of these patrons of the arts; when, before the power of the richest people in the country, the colors of the painting did not pale or a single form disappear; then these all-powerful lords sent their trusted employes, the executors of their peremptory orders, to deal drastically with the situation.

I preserve a beautiful memory of this "Battle of Rockefeller Center." A mysterious warlike atmosphere made itself felt from the very morning of the day that hostilities broke out. The private police patrolling the Center had already been reinforced during the preceding week, and on that day their number was again doubled. Towards eleven o'clock in the morning, the commander-in-chief of the building and his subordinate generals of personnel issued orders to the uniformed porters and detectives on duty to deploy their men and to begin occupying the important strategic positions on the front line and flanks and even behind the little working shack erected on the mezzanine floor which was the headquarters of the defending cohorts. The siege was laid in strict accordance with the best military practice. The lieutenants ordered their forces not to allow their line to be flanked nor to permit entrance to the beleaguered fort to anyone besides the painter and his assistants (five men and two women!) who constituted the total strength of the army to be subdued and driven from its positions. And all this to prevent the imminent collapse of the existing social order! I wish I could have been equally optimistic!

Several days before, orders had been given out not to allow camera men to enter. They were now made even more stringent, and there was no doubt that the owners would under any circumstances try to prevent the publication of any reproduction of the fresco. Fortunately, Miss Lucienne Bloch, one of my assistants, was adroit enough to take a series of ten details, as well as one complete view, with a tiny Leica camera under the very noses of the enemy's spies, who were so efficient that they failed to notice it!

Throughout the day our movements were closely watched. At dinner time, when our forces were reduced to a minimum—only I, my Japanese assistant, Hideo Noda, my Bulgarian assistant, Stephen Dimitroff, and the Swiss-American, Lucienne Bloch, were on duty—the assault took place. Before opening fire, and simultaneously with the final maneuvers which occupied the strategic posts and reinforced those already occupied, there presented himself, in all the splendor of his power and glory, and in keeping with the best gentlemanly traditions of His Majesty's Army, the great capitalist plenipotentiary, Field-Marshal of the contractors, Mr. Robertson, of Todd, Robertson and Todd, surrounded by his staff. Protected by a triple line of men in uniform and civilian clothes, Mr. Robertson invited me down from the scaffold to parley discreetly in the interior of the working shack and to deliver the ultimatum along with the final check. I was ordered to stop work.

In the meantime, a platoon of sappers, who had been hidden in ambush, charged upon the scaffold, replaced it expertly with smaller ones previously prepared and held ready, and then began to raise into position the large frames of stretched canvas with which they covered the wall. The entrance to the building was closed off with a thick heavy curtain (was it also bullet-proof?), while the streets surrounding the Center were patrolled by mounted policemen and the upper air was filled with the roar of airplanes flying round the skyscraper menaced by the portrait of Lenin. . . .

Before I left the building an hour later, the carpenters had already covered the mural, as though they feared that the entire city, with its banks and stock exchanges, its great buildings and millionaire residences, would be destroyed utterly by the mere presence of an image of Vladimir Ilyitch. . . .

The proletariat reacted rapidly. Half an hour after we had evacuated the fort, a demonstration composed of the most belligerent section of the city's workers arrived before the scene of battle. At once the mounted police made a show of their heroic and incomparable prowess, charging upon the demonstrators and injuring the back of a seven-year-old girl with a brutal blow of a club. Thus was won the glorious victory of Capital against the portrait of Lenin in the Battle of Rockefeller Center. . . .

But it was not yet over. If it is true that it is highly improbable that many of the seven million inhabitants of New York City would have seen the dangerous painting, on the other hand, thanks to the valiant attack of Capitalism against the mural, the press, the radio, the movies, all of the modern mediums of publicity, reported the event in the greatest detail over the entire territory of a country peopled by 125,000,000 people and even in the smallest villages of the United States. Tens of millions of people were informed that the nation's richest man had ordered the veiling of the portrait of an individual named Vladimir Ilyitch Lenin, because a painter had represented him in a fresco as the Leader, guiding the exploited masses towards a new social order based on the suppression of classes, organization, love and peace among human beings, in contrast to the war, unemployment, starvation, and degeneration of capitalist disorder. . . .

Even now, a year later, I continue to receive publications from Europe, from South Africa, from the Far East, China and Japan, from India and Australia and South America, carrying the same message to all the exploited workers in all parts of the world. Can Mr. Todd and Mr. Robertson ever calculate the number of exploited and oppressed proletarians who, thanks to their good offices, have been taught that in the opinion of the very overlords of America there is only one solution to the problems of hunger, unemployment, war, and all the cruel stages of capitalist crisis, and that this solution bears the name of Lenin?

The attack on the portrait of Lenin was merely a pretext to destroy the entire Rockefeller Center fresco. In reality, the whole mural was displeasing to the bourgeoisie. Chemical warfare, typified by hordes of masked soldiers in the uniforms of Hitlerized Germany; unemployment, the result of the crisis; the degeneration and persistent pleasures of the rich in the midst of the atrocious sufferings of the exploited toilers—all these symbolized the capitalist world on one of the crossed roads. On the other road, the organized Soviet masses, with their youth in the vanguard, are marching towards the development of a new social order, trusting in the light of History, in the clear, rational, omnipotent method of dialectical materialism, strong in their productive collectivization and in their efforts for the abolition of social classes by means of the necessary and logical proletarian dictatorship, result of the social revolution. This was expressed without demagogy or fantasy, with a simple objective painting of one of those marvelous mass demonstrations in the Red Square, under the shadow of the Kremlin and the Tomb of Lenin, which year after year give to the entire world an unequalled spectacle which makes visible and tangible the revolutionary march of the 160,000,000 inhabitants of the Soviet Union towards a better world. That road, too, is painful, hard, and filled with difficulties, but it leads ever forward, despite all the political vicissitudes inevitable in any revolutionary movement, to a more logical, juster, and more efficient human society, towards that time in which the period of "prehistory" will come to its end and, with the beginning of Communism, true human history will begin.

In the painting, Lenin, the Leader, unites in a gesture of permanent peace the hands of the soldier, the Negro farmer, and the white worker, while in the background the mass of workers with their fists held high affirm the will to sustain this fact; in the foreground, a pair of young lovers and a mother nursing her newborn child see in the realization of Lenin's vision the sole possibility of living, growing, and reproducing in love and peace. In the center, Man, the intelligent and producing skilled worker, controls vital energy and captures it for his own uses through the machine and by means of his knowledge of the life of the vast inter-stellar spaces and of the immensity of microbiologic space; while the mechanized hand, symbol of human power in action, grasps within its fingers the vital sphere—atoms and the cell, which are the essential reality of all life.

Two enormous lenses placed at the sides magnify these central elements of the composition for the eyes of the students and workers ranged in seated groups on each side of the main panel; these groups are made up of international types—Anglo-Saxons, Germans, Latins, Scandinavians, Indians, Jews, and Negroes—thus expressing the reality of the population of this continent, a continent peopled by numerous delegations of all the races of humanity, to realize in the future the synthetic human compound divested of racial hates, jealousies, and antagonisms, the synthesis that will give birth to intelligent and producing Man, master, at last, of the earth, and enjoying it in the high knowledge of creative energy and without the exploitation of his fellows.

"Too realistic," I was told. I can well believe it! That is why it did not suit the owners of the building. Had it not been realistic it would not have annoyed them; unable to deny the too evident reality of every day and hour, they hypocritically cover it with a veil.

"We were expecting that, in accordance with the theme, the work would be highly imaginative." Naturally! Thus you could have admitted everything in the name of "art," that mysterious prostitute which, unfortunately, has not for you the same meaning that it had for the Greeks, but is merely a curtain of fog, a luxurious and ridiculous robe behind which you can hide the disgusting sores of your decayed capitalist regime; of a piece with opium, cocaine, religion, and stupefying beverages, with which to drug and destroy, if possible, the intelligence and virility of men, to exploit them more easily as slaves so long as they are docile, and kill them like cattle in the slaughter house when it suits your interests. . . .

A few months later, Mr. Frank Brangwyn, who had been chosen to fill the walls originally intended for Matisse in the same building, found himself threatened with a conflict for having included the figure of Christ in his mural of the Sermon on the Mount. This time, the owners of the building, it appeared, did not consider that the atmosphere of a commercial enterprise was a fit environment for the Savior. The always curious newspaper men again sought me out to inquire my opinion of the new controversy. I answered that it was a manifestation of certain laws of history that in 1933, the nineteen hundredth anniversary of the expulsion of the money changers from the Temple by Jesus of Nazareth, the money changers should now be taking a belated revenge by expelling Jesus from their own Temple.

Unfortunately, the Brangwyn incident never attained great proportions, which is a pity, for it had elements of real comedy. When his mural illustration in oil of the Sermon on the Mount was pasted on the wall, Christ appeared with his back turned to the public, and the capitalists, like good Christians, not having to look the Lord in the face, were probably satisfied with this ingenious solution.

With the Rockefeller money (that is to say, with the money extorted from the workers by the Rockefeller exploiters), I painted a series of twenty-one panels in fresco in the New Workers' School of New York. The Rockefellers thought to prevent my talking to the people by destroying the fresco in their Center. In reality, they succeeded only in clarifying, intensifying, and multiplying my expression.

I shall not speak at length here of that series of panels, which is the first affirmative outline of the Portrait of America which I have begun to paint. They are, moreover, fully explained by the text which my friend and comrade, Bertram D. Wolfe, Director of the New Workers' School, with whose collaboration the series was planned and carried out, has contributed to this book. I painted them for the workers of New York, and for the first time in my life, I worked among "my own"; for the first time, I painted on a wall which belonged to the workers, not because they own the building in which their school has its quarters, but because the frescoes are built on movable panels which can be transported with them to any place where their school and headquarters may be called to move. They all helped in the work, and there, in the modest premises of an old and dirty building in 14th Street, at the top of a steel staircase as steep as those of the pyramids of Uxmal or Teotihuacán, I found myself in what was, for me, the best place in the city. The work lasted six months. I did all that I could to make something that would be useful to the workers, and I have the technical and analytical certainty that those frescoes are the best that I have painted, the best constructed, the most correct in historical dialectic, the richest in materialistic synthesis, and, moreover, informed with the greatest enthusiasm and love that I am capable of feeling.

For these reasons, I offered them to the workers of New York and asked the comrades of the New Workers' School to be their depositories. They, and many thousand others, were happy in the arrangement, and they notified me that, in the name of the producing masses of the United States, they were naming me the first "People's Artist" of America. In other words, they socialized me, as is done in Russia with those intellectuals who are considered useful to the community at large. And so America, the true, producing America, paid me in advance this splendid price for the portrait which I am just beginning.

I hope that this portrait may be in some small degree useful to a few hundreds, or thousands, or as many as possible, of the millions of workers who, in the near future, will carry out the formidable task of transforming, by means of revolutionary struggle and proletarian dictatorship, the marvelous industry of the super-capitalist country into the basic machinery for the splendid functioning of the Union of Socialistic Soviet Republics of the American Continent.

Diego Rivera

Mexico City,
February, 1934.

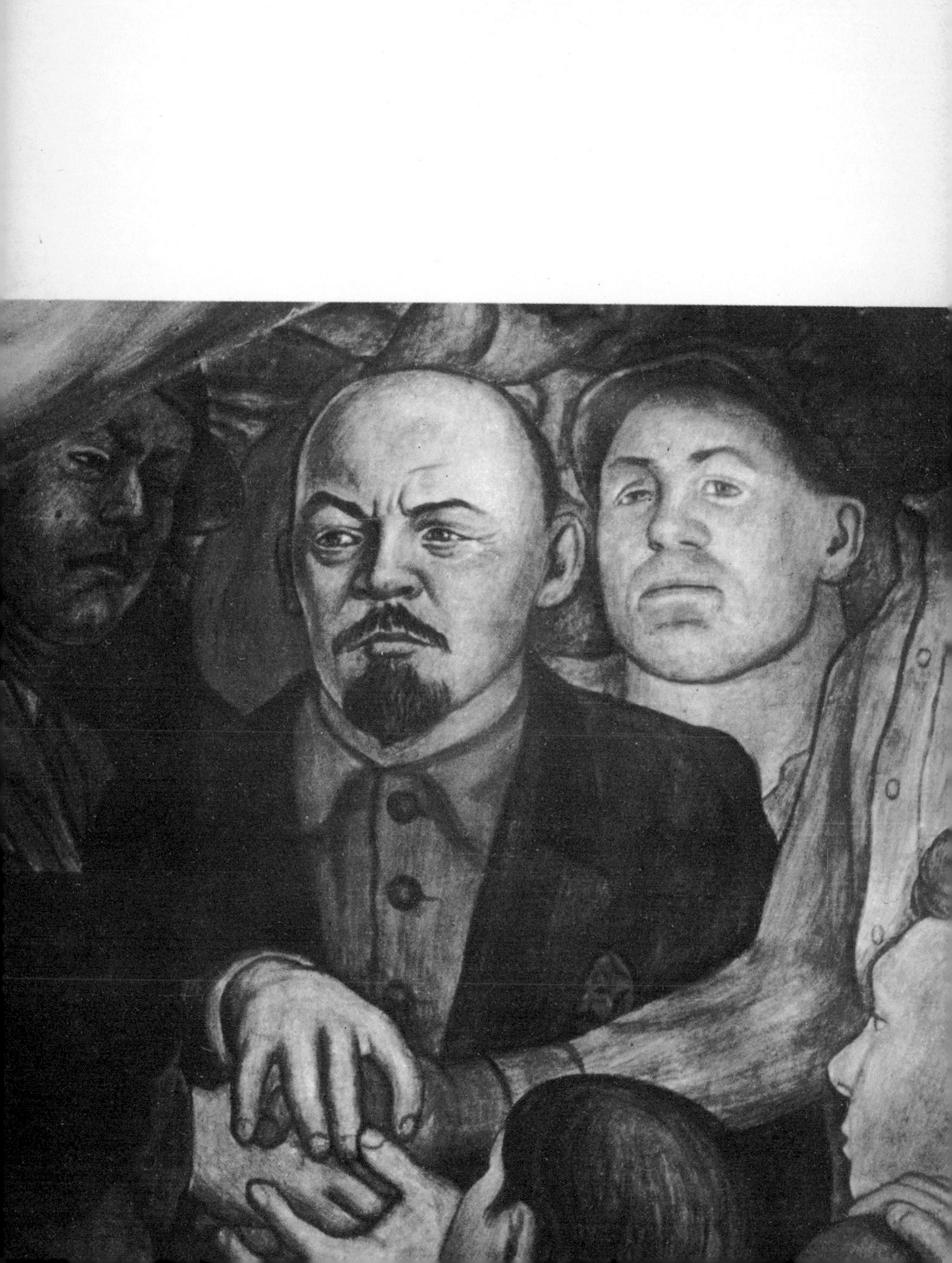

INDUSTRIAL AMERICA: PORTRAIT OF DETROIT

DIEGO RIVERA'S portrait of America really begins in Detroit. California was too like his native Mexico—its milder climate, its industries, mining and agriculture, its lingering traces of Spanish heritage. Moreover, there was his own newness to the land. But in Detroit he penetrated to the heart of the country, to its very foundation—modern, large-scale industry. The painter's esthetic delight in machinery, his militant interest in the social life of his time, were stirred profoundly by the industrial life of Detroit, and in the frescoes are the tempo, the stir, the noise, the movement, the labor, the dynamic, throbbing, crashing life of modern America.

The Detroit Institute of Arts is of "Renaissance" architecture, singularly inappropriate to a modern industrial city, an expression of the feeble tradition of imitative transplantation. Torn between the lesser necessity of adapting the painting to the building, and the greater of adapting it to the theme and the city whose life he was portraying, Rivera inevitably subordinated the first to the second. The doors, columns, window scrolls, etc., had, of course, to be taken into account, but the details of the building "ornamentation" have been played down, thus largely freeing the painting to adapt itself to the city, rather than the edifice. Where these details are too insistently obtrusive, the painting suffers accordingly. On the whole, however, the artist has been remarkably successful in his solution of this unavoidable conflict.

The painting occupies the entire four sides of the open inner court of the Detroit Institute of Arts, filling every available wall space with a series of 27 panels, the main ones of truly monumental proportions.

The painting is composed of three levels, determined by the structure of the walls and their ornamentation. The main wall space, from the base molding to the capital molding at the top of the columns is occupied by vast portrayals of machinery in motion and laborers at work, a foundry (page 62) and an automobile assembly plant (pages 65, 69, 70, 71). At their base are insets portraying incidents from a laborer's working day. Above the factory scenes, between moldings, there is a portrayal of the soil, subsoil, and physiography of the Detroit region, its minerals, its geological strata, its fossil remains, its lake and river location and transport, and between that and the rafters, symbolic portrayals of Nature's gifts, the races of men, and aviation.

The whole is bound together plastically by an undulating movement, marked by the moving belt conveyors, reflected in the wave-like geological strata and in the structural composition of the upper division, in the plastic "geometry" of every part of the painting. "As basic plan for the mural decoration," writes Rivera, "I chose the plastic expression of the wave-like movement which one finds in water currents, electric waves, stratifications of different layers under the surface of the earth, and, in a general way, throughout the continuous development of life."

Over the main entrance to the court (page 73) is portrayed water transportation which connects the industrial city with its distant sources of raw materials and markets.

Above this is aviation. On the left, airplane builders, performing autogenous, electric welding; in a small panel below, sunflowers constructed by nature in a form similar to the airplane motors, to resist the force of the wind, as the motor breaks through the resistance of the air; and a dove in flight in pursuit of an insect. On the right, military airplanes with aviators in gas masks; one, exhausted, has wrenched off his mask to breathe fresh, "untreated" air. The corresponding bird panel shows a hawk in pursuit of a smaller bird, maintaining itself by the destruction of weaker members of its own species—the painter seems to hint at imperialism as well as at the destruction of man by man in war.

Below, flanking the main entrance, are factory pipes, "stills" done with incredible tenderness—here is a painter who loves machinery.

In the upper section of the center (page 55) are workers' hands breaking through the crust of the earth and clasping pieces of mineral, tungsten, nickel, molybdenum, etc., the hard metals necessary for the production of steel. Below them are the crystalline formations characteristic of these metals (Rivera's quest for "models" carried him into the laboratories of Detroit, as in his paintings of bacteria and tissue cells at Radio City he found his "models" in the laboratories of the Rockefeller Institute—his "documentation" is reminiscent of the notebooks of a Leonardo da Vinci).

The two reclining figures, matched by two others on the opposite wall, are anthropomorphic analogs of the metals, and at the same time, representatives of the four races of man. Over iron and its related metals, is the figure of the red race; over coal strata and the crystalline diamond, a figure of the black race, and on the opposite wall (page 65) workers' hands taking silicon, soda, sulphur, lime, etc., from the bowels of the earth and representations of the yellow and the white races. The lack of "prettiness" in these four figures representing the four races is one of the counts in the indictment against Rivera's painting by those Detroit citizens who are agitating for the destruction of his murals.

The portrayal of the ferrous and carboniferous metals is surmounted by the crater of a volcano, nature's high-temperature blast furnace in which these crystals have been forged, echoed by a blast furnace in the huge portrayal of a foundry below.

Here Rivera is at his best: men at labor—our muscles tighten as we watch; machinery in motion—the curves and movements of pipes and chutes and belt conveyors provide a dynamic geometry that guides the vision, gives simplicity and organic unity to the profusion of detail and apparent confusion of a vast, ordered foundry, proportions the spaces and develops the movement of the painting. The wheels seem to go into motion on long gazing at the painting, the belts begin to travel; one can hear the hum and clatter and roar. For the first time the modern world has produced a modern painter capable of expressing its dynamism, catching the beauty of its machinery, the might of its labor, the glory of its mastery over the forces of nature, (and the tragic inadequacy of man's mastery over his own nature, over the organization of society).

This is not painting for the "art collector," pretty sentimentality for idle ladies and men-about-town, placid study of the texture and form and color of apples and bowls and flowers for the sensitive esthete.

In one of the insets on the opposite wall (page 67), Rivera has made an unusual use of the "moving picture" technique, a use which shows kinship with the experimentation of his cubist days when in association with Picasso and others he attempted to move around his object and fuse several successive appearances of it into a single image which "reconstitutes it in time and space." Here the "object" moves around in time and space while the painter or spectator watches. Two laborers rise and bend together in rhythmic movement and Rivera has put successive stages and geometrical forms and lines of their motion simultaneously into his painting, putting the technical skill acquired as a cubist at the service of motion in painting, or, as Rivera would phrase it, "dialectical materialism in esthetic technique."

No wonder the Detroit newspapers and outraged middle class guardians of the city's fair name and ornamentation found Rivera's work "disturbing instead of restful," "expressive of the darker side of life," "gloomy," "pessimistic" (this for the love of the machine and confidence in its future!) "uglifying instead of beautifying," even a "slander on the city." Had Rivera painted Detroit as a stately, impassive female figure of ample bosom and Romanesque drapery, with an automobile in one hand and a tractor in the other, surrounded by admiring and grateful sons and daughters, of magazine cover prettiness and fashionable dress (one of them might have worn overalls), the verdict of the same gentry would have been polite applause, and thereafter indifference. But no one can be indifferent to Rivera's Detroit, and one way or the other, the spectator is too moved to applaud.

THE CHURCH ATTACKS THE "HOLY FAMILY"

But the real storm broke over the painter, who seems fated to be a storm center wherever he goes, when certain ecclesiastics discovered his picture of a biological research laboratory where scientists are experimenting on useful, friendly animals to find vaccines for the protection of human life against the germs of disease and death that surround it.

The foreground of the panel reveals a child being vaccinated by a doctor assisted by a nurse, and surrounded by the three domesticated animals that are the chief source of vaccines: the horse, the sheep, and the cow. In this, the clerics found "blasphemy"!

There is an indubitable reminiscence of the Holy Family in this beautiful panel (page 59) : the animals in the stall where Christ was born; the suggestion of halo about the white cap of the nurse; the possibility of construing the nurse as the Virgin, the doctor as Joseph, perhaps even the three scientists as the three wise men.

Ever since the influential churchmen pronounced this beautiful work a piece of blasphemy, there has been continuous agitation for the destruction of the whole mural. Detroit has been libeled; all her citizens are shown at work—do they never play? The workers do not smile—does Rivera dare to insinuate that the citizens of God's own country's chosen city are not happy? The painting is sordid—do the citizens of Detroit do nothing but make material things? Detroit is portrayed as a center of industry, but what about Detroit as a cultural center? The gas masks are an implied, cynical criticism. The workers are all round-shouldered. Factories are ugly, why did not the painter choose the beautiful things in Detroit? But above all, sacrilege, blasphemy—the painter is mocking at our most sacred institutions.

When the Rockefellers destroyed the murals in Radio City, this brand of "esthetic criticism" received a new impetus. One thousand Catholic students at a Catholic Sodality Symposium, on February 22, 1934, resolved to boycott the Museum until Rivera's frescoes are removed and pledged themselves to "undying opposition to the Rivera murals in the Detroit Institute of Fine Arts."

Rivera's answer is characteristic, and illuminating as to the painter's own conception of the murals. In *Creative Art,* he writes:

"In consequence of its scientific and industrial development, this country is destined in the coming years to be the terrain of a conflict between two forces, the progressive and the static. My Detroit murals have brought into close proximity the two poles, positive and negative, with the resultant explosion. If my work must disappear, it will at least have served to bring out clearly these two opposing forces.

"It is noteworthy that the ecclesiastical powers evince little interest in art which is innocuously abstract or socially meaningless; even art which is sexually inciting may be pardoned—as can, at a variable tariff, the venial 'sins' it may inspire. But the only pure and true art—art which clarifies and formulates the realities of life—will always risk the ban of ecclesiastical powers which assert the right to aesthetic as well as 'spiritual' domination. Art in their hands is an instrument of oppression, just as it can, in other hands, become a weapon of emancipation.

"If my Detroit frescoes are destroyed, I shall be profoundly distressed, as I put into them a year of my life and the best of my talent; but tomorrow I shall be busy making others, for I am not merely an 'artist,' but a man performing his biological function of producing paintings, just as a tree produces flowers and fruit, nor mourns their loss each year, knowing that the next season it shall blossom and bear fruit again."

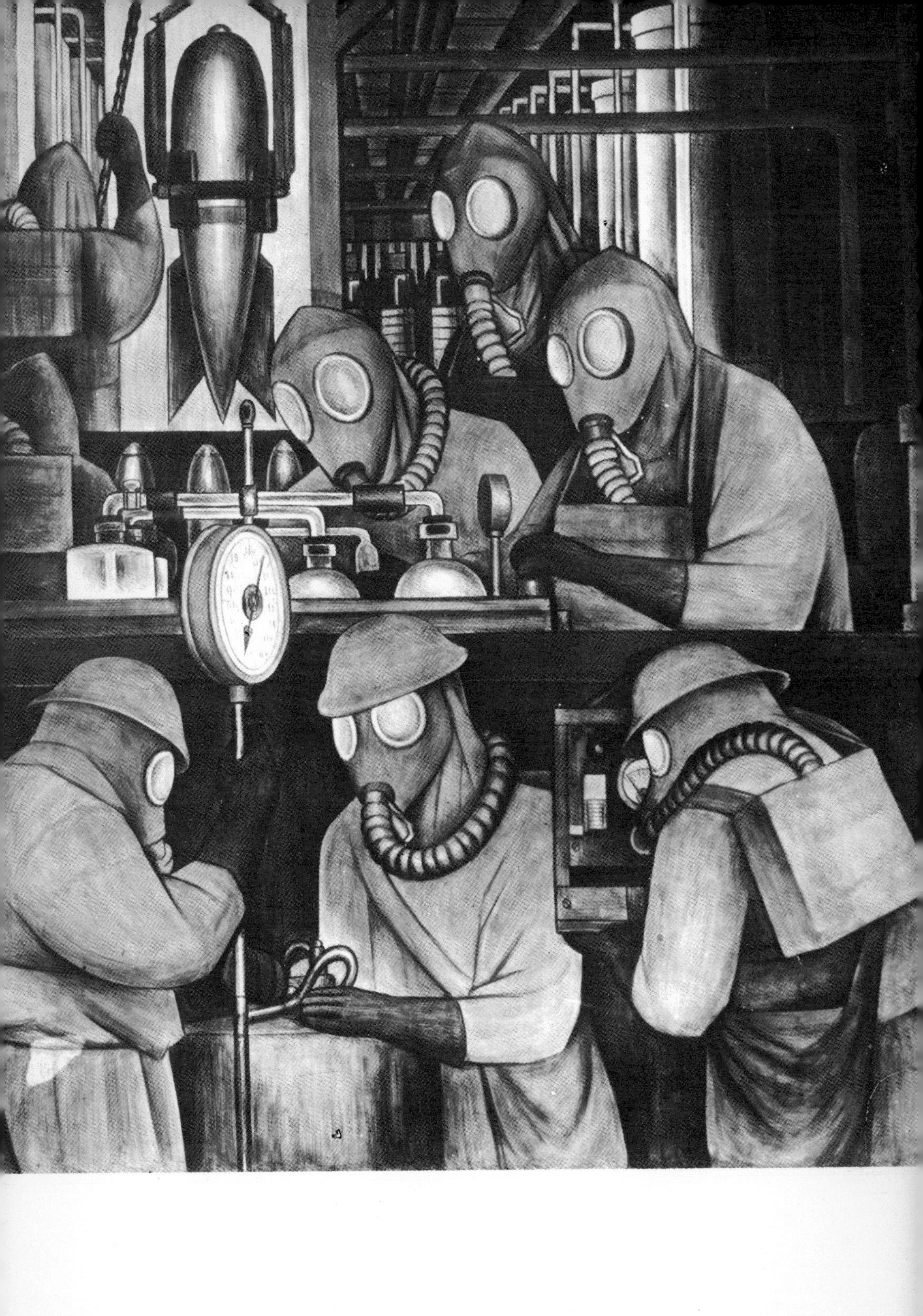

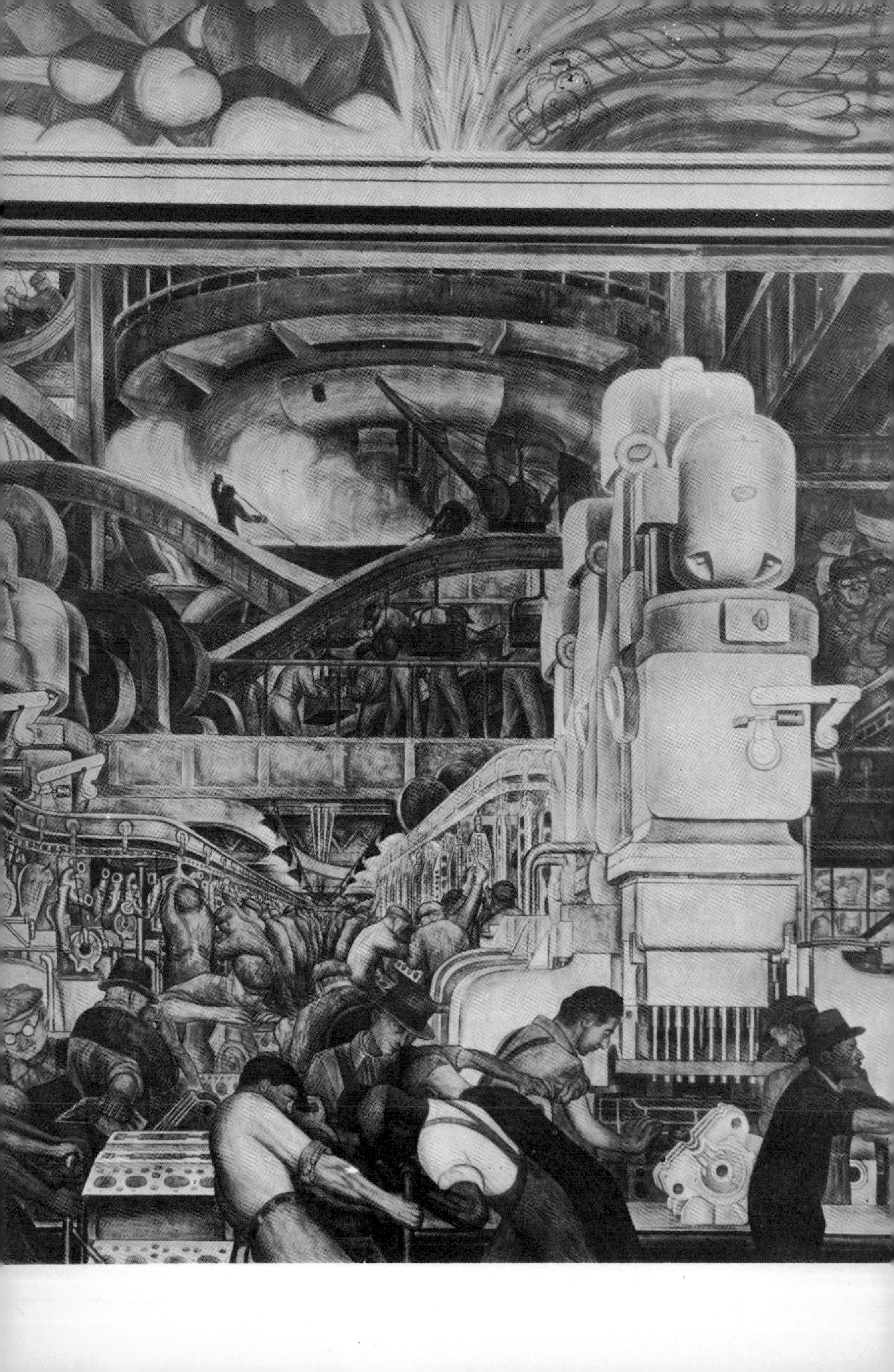

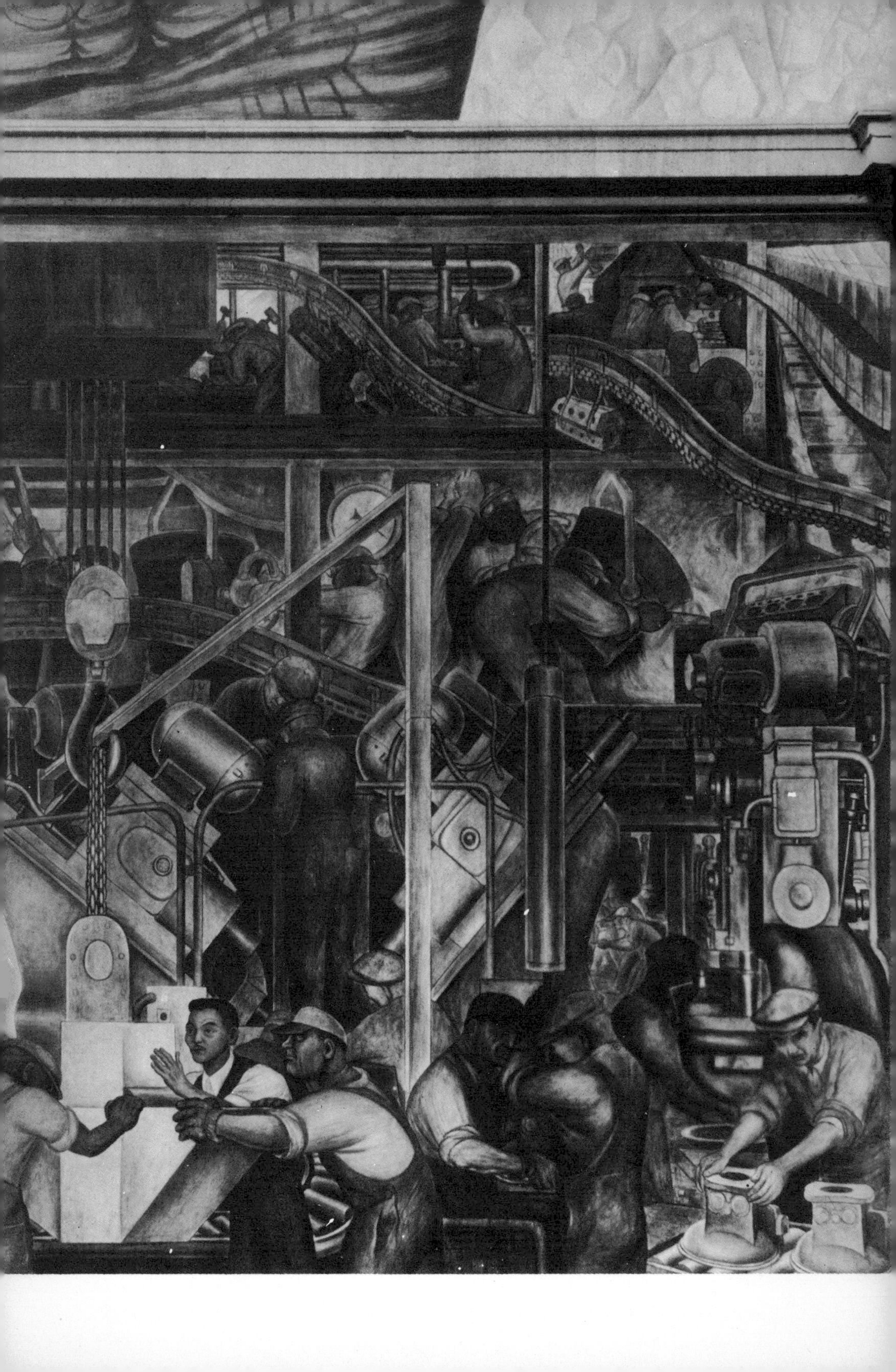

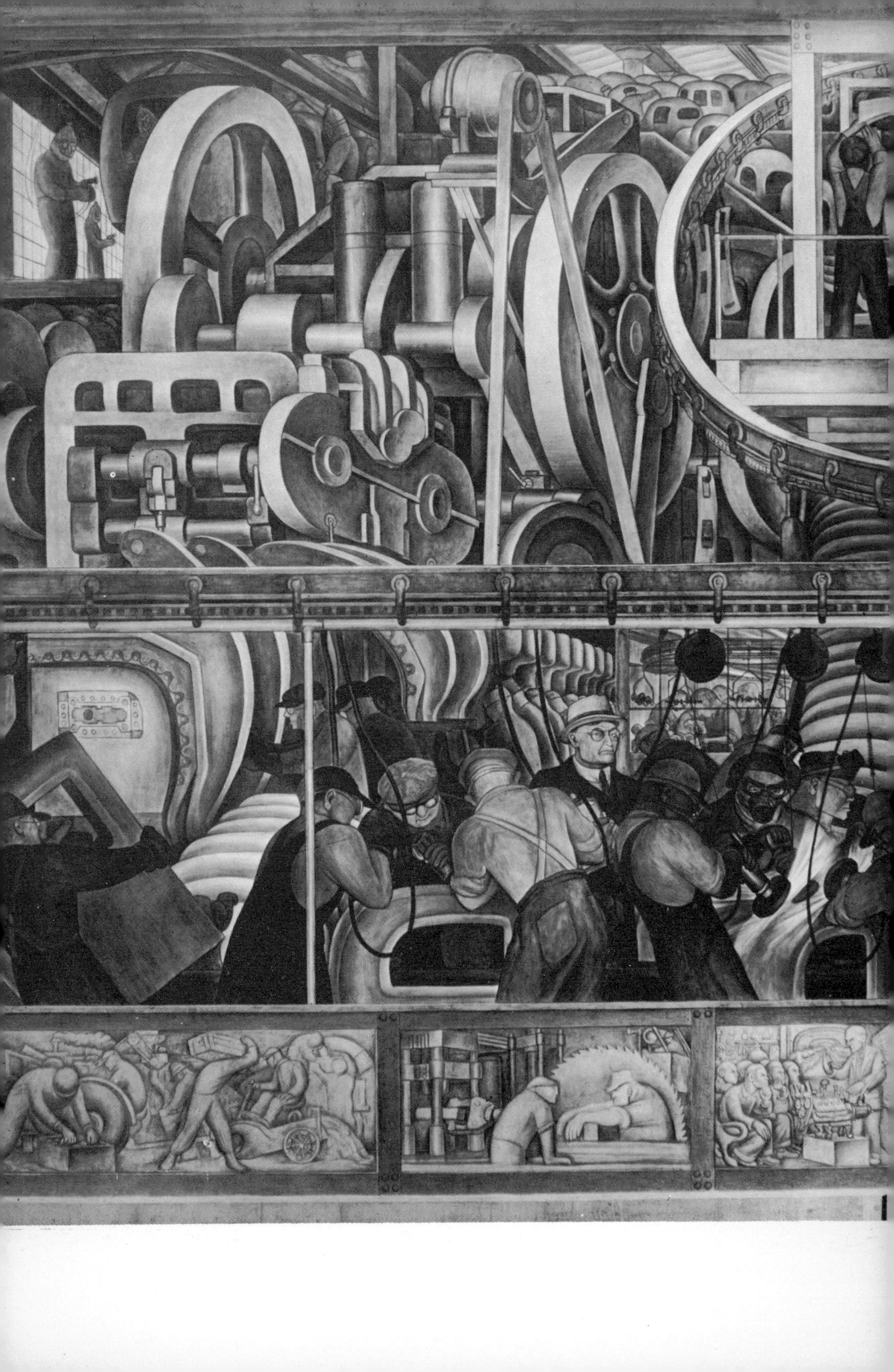

1

VITA BREVIS LONGA ARS

PORTRAIT OF AMERICA

"THE history of all human society . . . has been the history of class struggles." This dictum of Marx provides the dynamics of Diego Rivera's "Portrait of America." And in the very foundations of the imposing edifice of American capitalism—in colonial America—the painter reveals the beginnings of class division and class struggle.

THE CONQUERORS

The discovery of America, its exploration and its settlement, were by-products of the disintegration of European feudalism. Medieval society, intact in the thirteenth century, was in fragments by the seventeenth. The growth of commerce and merchant capital, a revolutionary force, created cities, promoted travel, taught geography, developed navigation, astronomy and other sciences, expanded the limits of the earth and made heaven more remote.

Trade changed products into commodities; it changed gold and silver from articles of adornment into the representative of all things on earth, not to mention heaven. Money replaced payment in kind and feudal service, dissolved feudal relations, expanded the limits of exploitation, created a hunger for gold, a hunger for land, a hunger for power.

The decline of feudalism brought with it the revolt of the knights, the driving of peasants off the land, the Peasants' Wars, the struggles of king and burghers against the nobility, wars for national economic unity, wars for overseas trade and colonial wars, a split in the universal church, religious wars.

The quest for trade routes discovered America. The hunger for gold explored and conquered America. The dispossessing of the peasantry and the dislocation of economy settled America. Amidst the

death agonies of feudalism and the prolonged birth pangs of capitalism, America was discovered, conquered, peopled, by gold-hungry, trade-hungry, land-hungry, and just plain hungry Europeans.

THE CONQUERED

The background of the colonial panel shows the landing of settlers, the exploration of a river valley, and the dispossessing and despoiling of the Indians—an Indian village being burned, Indians being enslaved, a firing squad, Indian women being dragged away by soldiers.

The foreground shows the more "peaceful" relations of trade promoted by the three great "persuaders"—the leathern whiskey jug, the Bible and the blunderbus. The hands, as in all Rivera's work, are eloquent: the eager, trembling hand reaching for the "fire water," the formalistic, hypocritical hand administering a blessing, the careless hands from which a skin slides as if the Indian held material objects of little account, and the grasping, clutching hands of a trader. Four grim figures are here, representing the conquest in all its aspects, the missionary or priest, the whiskey-vendor, the trader and the soldier. Behind them stands yet a fifth medium of disintegration and conquest —the prostitute.

THE TRANSPORTED

Wealth and poverty are polar phenomena. Wealth at one pole requires poverty at the other. The European conquerers dreamt of establishing a new feudalism, but what good were the vast stretches of land taken from the Indians unless there was a surplus population without means of existence, who could be made to work the land for its owners? In colonial countries where vast stretches of land are unoccupied, it becomes necessary to "cast about for artificial means which will ensure the poverty of the common people." (Marx.) Hence, when chattel slavery was long outgrown in Europe and even feudalism was crumbling away, both were resorted to in colonial America.

First the conquerors attempted to enslave the Indians. In Mexico and Spanish America generally, slavery and modified feudalism (*la encomienda*) were feasible, for the tropical Indian had developed a settled habitation and a civilization with sufficient points of similarity to the economy of Europe. But the nomadic Redman of the Northern region refused to accept Christian submissiveness and enforced labor as a substitute for his ancient freedoms and his ancient possessions. When the Bible and brandy failed to "civilize" the Indian and persuade him to accept the ways and the chains of the Christian invader, then the blunderbus was used as the last and most convincing of the three. And so in time the proverb took root: "The only good Indian is a dead Indian"; and from treaty to treaty, from region to region, from reservation to reservation, from hunting ground to "happy hunting ground," the Indian was driven off his ancient heritage, the American land. But blunderbusses plough no fields and work no mines or mills—the "labor problem" was still unsolved. The conquerors still faced the problem of either working themselves or enslaving others.

THE WHITE SLAVES

Rivera has painted them coming from the ship—poor immigrants, indentured slaves, white Europeans who are to be bought and sold to work off their passage, to work off fines levied for vagrancy or begging, for the crime of being unemployed and dispossessed from the soil, to work off debts which are being punished by the alternative penalty of imprisonment or transportation to America.

They look weary as they disembark for the auction block. Their voyage has not been a pleasant one. They have been sailing two or three months under conditions of terrible misery, sickness, and horror, and never-ending hunger and thirst. Such are the beginnings of America's "free" white working class.

THE BLACK SLAVES

But they do not come fast enough! The new American ruling class

is endowed with a vast empire and is labor-hungry. White slaves are sold only for a term of years. The term ends and the slave develops—as one of the slave-holders complained—"a passion for owning land which prevents the existence of a class of laborers for hire." So the black slave was introduced.

A line of them is seen leaving the slave ship. Their trip has been even worse than that of the whites. There have been no legal forms preserved—they have simply been kidnapped. Throughout the voyage they have been in chains, between decks, packed so close "that there was no possibility of their lying down, or at all changing their position, by night or day. . . ." Perhaps a third of them have been tossed overboard on the way. Such is their introduction to Christian America!

There are two lines of slaves in the panel, one moving down from the boat to the foreground, and the other, men and women, naked to the waist, loading the ship with a cargo of things which Indians and the black and white slaves have produced in the New World.

In the middle background is the skyline of Dutch New York with glimpses of colonial industry: white laborers at work in the skilled trades, weaving, smithing, carpentry; black men in the fields and at heavy labor; and red men fishing in the stream. In the center stands the slave market, as it stands in the center of colonial economy.

Dominating the middle ground of the picture is the sinister figure of the white master punishing the rebellious slave. For those Africans who can be civilized and taught to accept American institutions, there is the pedagogy of the whipping post. And for those who are incurably rebellious and unteachable, there is the hangman's noose.

What are the "positive" things that Rivera sees in colonial America? They are productive labor, always a creative force under any social system, the rebelliousness of the American Indian who will not be enslaved, and the rebelliousness of the Negro slave. Such are the first traditions for the American working class to remember and cherish.

"THE people who write histories are usually of the class who take the side of the government in a revolution; and as Americans, they are anxious to believe that our revolution was different from others, more decorous, and altogether free from the atrocities, mistakes, and absurdities which characterize even the patriot party in a revolution. They have accordingly tried to describe a revolution in which all scholarly, refined and conservative persons might have unhesitatingly taken part; but such revolutions have never been known to happen." So writes S. G. Fisher in his *True History of the American Revolution.*

But Rivera's portrayal of the American Revolution is one which those good Tory ladies of our day, the Daughters of the American Revolution, could never accept as an ancestral achievement.

A "REVOLUTIONARY REVOLUTION"

Rivera has portrayed a revolutionary revolution: one preceded and inspired by agitation and propaganda; carried on by boycott, demonstration, mass action and force of arms; directed by conspirative organizations and "unconstitutional," extra-legal bodies, created by the American as by all revolutions to mobilize its forces for resistance to the legal authority and form the germ of the revolutionary dictatorship and future government if the uprising should succeed.

THE MEN OF THE REVOLUTION

Hence Rivera has selected as his central figures, the three outstanding propagandists of the American Revolution, Benjamin Franklin, Thomas Paine (in the foreground of Panel II), and Thomas Jefferson (in Panel III), and the outstanding organizer of the extra-legal apparatus of mobilization and dictatorship, Sam Adams (in front of the Independence Hall group at the right of Panel II).

LIBERTY TREE
STAMP ACT
THE FOLLY OF ENGLAND
THE RUIN OF AMERICA

To Benjamin Franklin and Thomas Paine, as the reader will observe by their position and the loving care with which the painter has delineated their thoughtful faces and dream-filled eyes, Rivera attaches special significance. It is they who symbolize the international historic significance of the American struggle, which made it, as the first of the modern bourgeois revolutions, the precursor and inspirer of the Great French Revolution. Rivera's Benjamin Franklin is the great commoner drawn from the stock of the plain people, who matched wits with Pennsylvania's aristocrats, with England's lawyers, and France's courtiers; the 18th century rationalist with open, free, curious mind, testing all things, examining all things in the light of bourgeois reason; the economist who advocated agrarianism, populism, laissez-faire, labor theory of value and paper currency; the self-taught natural philosopher and scientist; the incorruptible democrat who rejected a thousand bribes, disowned a son for accepting a royal governorship, and raised a solitary voice in the Constitutional Convention for universal suffrage, a single-chamber legislature, and a government responsible to the people; the free-thinking deist; the first provincial American to attain to a cosmopolitan mind and influence; the democratic, progressive, middle-class incarnation of that third estate which made the bourgeois revolutions of America and Europe.

Thomas Paine, "that filthy little atheist," as Theodore Roosevelt so gratefully described him in token of his services to the American Revolution, is an even more attractive figure to Rivera. In his hand is a scroll, to which both Franklin and he are pointing, in explanation to representative mass figures that surround them. The scroll bears the titles of two of his works, and characteristic utterances:

"My country is the World; to do good is my religion," a reminder of the militant free-thinking and cosmopolitan internationalism that made this Englishman come to America in December 1774 to join the colonial struggle for freedom, and then leave for France to participate in the French Revolution, albeit as a Girondin. And his populism finds burning expression in the most modern-sounding of his words:

"The contrast of affluence and wretchedness is like dead and living bodies chained together."

THE ORGANIZER OF THE REVOLUTION

It is characteristic of this series of murals that Rivera generally designates his central figures not merely by position but also by the presence of a scroll or a finger or hand pointing the way. As Paine holds the scroll, so Sam Adams shows his leading role by a pointing hand. He is the "People's Tribune," the man of the Town Meeting, the organizer of the Revolution. Skilled in urging forward the whole slow-moving mass, seeing far beyond it but never running too far ahead of it, he carried the struggle from the town meeting to the legislature, from the legislature by circular letter to the other colonies, and inaugurated the Committees of Correspondence and Committees of Safety which were the party machinery and Jacobin Clubs and "local soviets" of the American Revolution. It was by these Committees of Correspondence and Committees of Public Safety, the Circular Letters and pledges, the Stamp Act Congress and Continental Congresses, the illegally meeting dissolved legislatures, the Sons of Liberty, Minute Men and illegal militias, that the forces of the Revolution were organized and the dual authority constituted that first challenged the existing government and then seized power and became the revolutionary government—Congress, legislatures and Continental Army. Sam Adams, so consistently neglected by Federalist-prejudiced historians, is selected by Rivera as representative of this organizing development.

THE TREATMENT OF WASHINGTON

Washington and other "fathers of the country," who were part of the colonial ruling class and later formed the Federalist Party and ruling class of the new Republic, appear only in the background. In the center of the uppermost portion of the panel, Washington is shown still part of the British colonial apparatus, as a colonel in the French and Indian Wars, lifting his hat to a British Flag which he has just raised over a captured French fort. On the right, still in the remote background, Rivera has portrayed Mount Vernon as symbol of the fruits of the junior partnership of wealthy colonials in British rule. Here Washington is shown overseeing the labor of slaves in his fields. And on the extreme right of Panel III, he appears again as the chief opposing figure to Daniel Shays. In response to a question by a reporter on his treatment of the figure of Washington, Rivera explained:

"I do not consider Washington as a central revolutionary figure although I recognize his great significance as a leader and organizer of the American War for Independence. He is a figure somewhat similar to Iturbide in Mexico. He was an officer of the British colonial army and a part of the British colonial apparatus, who went over to a revolutionary position when he saw the native colonial ruling class, of which he was a part, hampered by the restrictions of the ruling class of the metropolis. His understanding of the American Revolution was limited to that, and therefore he played a thoroughly conservative and even reactionary role in the social changes arising out of the revolution and construction of a new government."

THE EVENTS OF THE REVOLUTION

The dynamic movement in the panel is not secured through the portrayal of the leaders, but through the action of the masses and the clash of opposing governmental and popular forces. Again Rivera has selected incidents calculated to reveal the revolutionary nature of the whole struggle. A colonial who has accepted the hateful post of tax collector has been tarred and feathered by the Sons of Liberty and is being ridden on a cart through the town. Rebellious townspeople, disguised fittingly as unsubduable, liberty-loving Indians, are dumping the tea into Boston Harbor. And as the center of the panel, Rivera has selected the Boston Massacre, showing the clash of forces involved in the whole period. The masses here appear demonstrating under their own popular leaders, headed by Crispus Attucks, escaped Southern Negro slave, one of the four victims of the Boston Massacre.

The whole composition is designed to bring out the same clash of forces. The line of oppression and tyranny carries over from the cat-o'-nine tails in the hands of the slave-driver in Panel I, through the line of the yardarm of the tea ship, the Union Jack and the line of firing soldiers, and ends in the figure of the captured tax collector. Completely surrounding and engulfing this "line of tyranny" is the "line of rebellion"—directly under the yardarm, the tea party; confronting the soldiers, demonstrating masses, a raised club, a clenched fist; around the tax collector, and filling the foreground, the populace, the agitators, and the Sons of Liberty; on the right-hand side, more demonstrators, the organizer, and the proclamation of the Declaration of Independence; over all, serving as a visual support for the roof of the hall in which the murals are walls, and running even into the next panel, the Liberty Tree. The remote background continues the landscape of America and portrays the French and Indian Wars, background out of which the American Revolution developed.

There is a flavor of contemporary authenticity about the central scenes, for Rivera's Boston Massacre is plainly inspired in Paul Revere's colored engraving of the same incident (Revere was artist, printer, engraver and dentist, among other things, besides being the hero of his celebrated ride), and the tarred and feathered tax collector comes from a contemporary woodcut. The rest of the iconography, here as throughout the panels, is likewise from contemporary sources.

PANEL III REVOLUTION AND REACTION: SHAYS' REBELLION

EVERY popular revolution, upon examination, reveals itself to be the movement of several classes with a variety of conceptions as to the ultimate aims of the struggle. The success of a revolution immediately results in a class differentiation with a consequent differentiation of programs and wings.

The American Revolution is no exception. The most conservative class involved was the financial-commercial-land-speculator big bourgeoisie, whose spokesmen were the aristocratic Washington, chief stockholder of the Ohio Land Company; the monarchical-plutocratic Hamilton, impecunious devotee of the "rule of the rich and the well-born"; the "mob-hating" John Adams who urged monarchy upon the newly freed country and undertook the successful defense of the eight soldiers accused of the Boston massacre; the financier Robert Morris; and all those who later drafted the Constitution (with the exception of Franklin), set up the institutions of the Federal Government, and founded the Federalist Party. These are the figures whom conservative historians have celebrated in their panegyrics. But Rivera, viewing the first American Revolution from the standpoint of those who would make the second, thrusts these leaders into the background or omits them entirely, as so many historians with less reason of space and none of historic objectivity have omitted Samuel Adams and Daniel Shays.

To the political left of Washington and Hamilton and John Adams, we find Franklin, Paine, Sam Adams, Patrick Henry, and Jefferson. They are the Robespierres, Marats, and Saint Justs of the American Revolution, and Rivera gives them due importance as the main organizers and propagandists and inspirers of the War for Independence and the democratic movement growing out of it. Thomas Jefferson is here as the aristocrat with agrarian-populist tendencies; as the champion of the inconsistent, and in the long run hopeless, battle of the petty-bourgeoisie and agrarian elements against centralized government and concentrated industrial and banking capital; as the political philosopher of the Revolution; as the representative of the current that forced the Bill of Rights into an otherwise reactionary Constitution; and as the author of the Declaration of Independence. The Declaration he drafted was far more than a mere announcement of separation and statement of grievances, more even than a statement of democratic political philosophy along the line of the social contract theory of Locke and Rousseau. Its pivotal point is the theory of the right of revolution. For Rivera and the working class today, as for Jefferson when he wrote it, the central "self-evident" truth, the most truly immortal words of that "immortal" document are the ones which assert:

"whenever any form of government becomes destructive of these ends, it is the right of the people to alter or to abolish it."

THE FORGOTTEN JEFFERSON

That Jefferson really believed in this permanent right of the people to revolution is proved by his subsequent reaction to the Shays movement and the Whiskey Rebellion. It is not the Declaration of Independence, trotted out every fourth of July by conservative orators and ignored the other 364 days of the year, that Rivera has put into the hands of Jefferson, but his seldom quoted words on Shays' Rebellion:

"God forbid, that we should ever be twenty years without such a rebellion. . . . What country can preserve its liberties, if its rulers are not warned from time to time, that the people preserve the spirit of resistance . . . ?

"Let them take arms. What signify a few lives lost? The tree of Liberty must be refreshed from time to time with the blood of patriots and tyrants."

Don't Tread
On Me
COURT HOUSE
SLAVES MARKET
MASONIC TEMPLE
THE TREE OF LIBERTY MUST
BE REFRESHED FROM TIME TO TIME
WITH THE BLOOD OF PATRIOTS
AND TYRANTS

The American Revolution was in the first place a revolt against a colonial system which limited the further development of colonial forces of production, denied the colonists the right to manufacture what they pleased, settle where they pleased, trade where they could buy most cheaply and sell most profitably, decide the incidence and expend as they pleased the revenues raised by taxation, and govern themselves in the interests of their own economy, and not that of the mother country. These restrictions, once harmless and even protective, had been outgrown and had changed into fetters upon further growth. Thus the American Revolution was more than a mere "war for independence," it was a social movement against absolutism and mercantile-feudal encumbrances. As such, it inspired the French Revolution and awoke an echo throughout Europe, not excluding England.

From all over Europe liberal aristocrats, moved by various combinations of love of freedom and hatred of England, came to America to aid the cause of freedom. Rivera has painted them near Washington and Hamilton, but it is obvious that his Lafayette, Kosciusko, DeKalb and Von Steuben, are regarded with little sympathy by the artist. They aided the cause of freedom, but within that cause they strengthened the aristocratic, conservative right.

The Revolution received the support not only of free-lance liberal aristocrats and British Whigs, but of the French absolute monarchy and other opponents of England as well. Rivera has portrayed this in the remote background of the panel which continues the American landscape, shows on the left the mass actions of guerilla warfare on the frontier, women fighting shoulder to shoulder with the men, in the center a woman reminiscent of Molly Pitcher loading a cannon, and on the right, the battle of Yorktown won through the cooperation of the French fleet and the army.

As a social movement, the Revolution disestablished the Anglican Church and weakened the others, proclaimed religious toleration, abolished proprietary and royal dues and prerogatives, wiped out quit-rent and primogeniture and other vestiges of feudalism, confiscated and broke up Tory estates, smashed the Proclamation Line, paving the way for Westward expansion and the establishment of a numerous small proprietor farmer class as the foundation of the Agrarian-Populist movement which achieved temporary triumph in the Jeffersonian and Jacksonian and Civil War radical democratic movements, and which has been fighting a losing battle against railroads, trusts, and banks ever since. It dealt a death blow to absolutism and mortally wounded Toryism in England, and made a breach in the shaky system of mercantilist economic politics and feudal survivals, embodied in classic form in the *Ancien Régime* in France.

AIMS OF THE LEFT

But like all bourgeois revolutions, it embodied social aspirations far beyond those actually realized. These aspirations served to enlist popular support. They were vaguely stated: "All men are created equal"; "right to life, liberty and the pursuit of happiness." Jefferson even envisaged the abolition of slavery and listed the implantation of the slave system as one of the grievances against the King of England, but this clause of the Declaration was stricken out upon the floor of Congress.

As soon as English rule was broken, a struggle began as to which course the revolutionary reconstruction was to take. The wage-earners and petty-bourgeois democrats demanded universal suffrage. The westerners demanded free access to the land they had won from the British. The heavily indebted farmers demanded paper money. The demobilized soldiers, mostly poor farmers, demanded pay. And when they returned, they found that their lands had been seized for debt, and that

GOD FORBID, THAT WE SHOULD EVER
BE TWENTY YEARS WITHOUT
SUCH A REBELLION.
WHAT COUNTRY CAN PRESERVE ITS
LIBERTIES, IF ITS RULERS ARE NOT
WARNED FROM TIME TO TIME, THAT
THE PEOPLE PRESERVE THE SPIRIT
OF RESISTANCE?
LET THEM TAKE ARMS.
WHAT SIGNIFY A FEW LIVES LOST?
THE TREE OF LIBERTY MUST
BE REFRESHED FROM TIME TO TIME
WITH THE BLOOD OF PATRIOTS
AND TYRANTS.

they themselves had fought for freedom only to win a debtor's prison. For the Washingtons and Hamiltons, the revolution had gone too far. They aimed at reaction and the rule of financiers, merchants, land speculators, and planter aristocracy. For the Jeffersons and Franklins and Patrick Henrys, the revolution needed rounding off and consolidation, as a moderate, agrarian democracy, but had gone just about far enough. For the masses, the revolution was still in its initial stages. This movement of the poor farmers, wage-earners, and debtors to complete the social program of the revolution reached its high point in Shays' Rebellion (1786) which Rivera has made the center of the panel.

Of its vague equalitarian principles, General Knox wrote to Washington:

"Their creed is, that the property of the United States has been protected from the confiscation of Britain by the joint exertions of all, and therefore ought to be the common property of all. . . ."

The immediate program of these revolutionary farmers, wearing sprigs of fir as badges in their hats, carrying rifles they had used to free the country from England, fighting under a revolutionary captain, was far more moderate than their principles as stated by the frightened Knox. They wanted inflation, a moratorium on debts, the cessation of foreclosures and imprisonment for debt, popular control of the legislature and courts, and a popular militia. Constituting a majority in the state, they prevented foreclosure sales by attending the sessions of the courts in mass, much as the western farmers did during 1933.

THE CONSTITUTION

"This dreadful situation," continues General Knox's letter, "has alarmed every man of principle and property in New England. . . . Our Government must be braced, changed, or altered to secure our lives and property."

Hastily the men of "principle and property" were mobilized to defend property, principle, and interest. The movement spread rapidly to other states. Under the pretext of raising troops against the Indians, Congress in secret session voted to raise an army under General Lincoln to crush Shays' Rebellion and similar movements in other parts of the country. To raise funds, "a number of wealthy gentlemen" were induced to "advance a part of their property in order to save the rest." And a conspiracy was hatched to scrap the Articles of Confederation and adopt a new Constitution.

Rivera has depicted the opposing forces of this final stage of the revolution as personified by Washington and Hamilton and their aristocratic entourage on the one side, and Shays followed by his men on the other. The new Star-Spangled Banner is borne by soldiers but lately in the Revolution, against their comrades-in-arms. Shays' men bear the earlier revolutionary red flag with its pine-tree and rattlesnake and the motto, "Don't Tread on Me."

To the left, behind the red flag, is a concentrated representation of a revolutionary headquarters, where meetings are being held, manifestoes edited and printed, and powder and shot being made. It carries over from the preceding panel as the symbol of revolutionary unity against England. It contrasts with the buildings on the right, court house, slave market, masonic temple and church, symbols of the consolidation of the new ruling class and Federalist reaction under the Constitution.

The crushing of Shays' Rebellion in 1786 meant the victory of the financial aristocracy under Washington and Hamilton, and the formation of a conservative, bourgeois republic, where popular representation, minimized by property qualifications, is further hamstrung by a unique system of checks and balances by senate, president and courts upon the only chamber even semi-popular in character. Rivera has placed the slave market once more in the center of this panel, symbol of its central role in the economy of the new Republic.

IN the foundations of America were two contradictory principles. One was that of the Declaration of Independence, with its theory of democratic equality, responsible government, and the right of revolution, and its offspring, the Bill of Rights, the Northwest Ordinance, Jeffersonian and Jacksonian Democracy. The other was that of the Constitution, with its distrust of the masses, its checks upon the will of the people, its rejection of universal suffrage, its acceptance of slavery, and its conception of government as the guardian of property rights, with its lusty progeny, the national debt, banking, the protective tariff, the factory system, Federalism, Whiggism, and the long line of plutocratic rule and concentration of wealth ranging from Hamilton to Andrew Mellon, from debt-assumption to the compulsive combinations in restraint of trade and the price-lifting of the NRA. One was the aspiration of the petty-bourgeoisie; the other of the great bourgeoisie. They were contradictory principles, yet often they reinforced each other, for they had this in common—they were both dreams of a bourgeois America, and, given the economic conditions of the time, no other dream could be realized. Therefore, the big bourgeoisie as the representative of the progressive drive for national unity and expansion of economy often took the petty-bourgeoisie in tow. It was Hamilton and not Jefferson who in the long run was destined to shape America; and so Rivera in the panel showing the building of the new edifice, has omitted Jefferson altogether and given Hamilton and Polk the key positions.

CLASH OF DREAMS

Yet there was much argument of architects and Babel of builders in the building of America—conflict of plans and clash of dreams. Here is Emerson, flanked by Margaret Fuller and Thoreau, pointing out to

"THE REANNEXATION OF TEXAS; THE
REOCCUPATION OF OREGON; FIFTY-FOU
FORTY OR FIGHT!"

a few simple folk the way to a transcendental Utopia. Here is Houston, flanked by Brigham Young and Austin, pointing westward. Here is Polk with his hand grasping the Oregon territory and the Mexican cession. Here is Morse, painter who has forsaken his palette for another art, the art of invention, brooding on the day when the machine shall communicate and multiply the thoughts of men, abolish poverty, give victory in the animal struggle with nature, produce plenty and leisure and opportunity for culture for all mankind. And solidly planted before the national bank stands Hamilton, dreaming of boundless wealth, factory smokestacks, child and woman labor, the rule of the rich and the well-born. In front of him stand the prototypes of the money kings, John Jacob and William B. Astor, shrewdly dreaming of personal piles of yellow metal, self-accumulating wealth, monopoly, and power. Before them stands Old Hickory, scowling and puzzled at forces too mighty for his simple statecraft, dreaming grimly of smashing the money power and keeping the government in the hands, not of the workers and farmers, for he has the petty-bourgeois inability to understand class forces, but of "the plain people." Amid such argument among the architects, amid such varied and contradictory dreaming, the structure of the mighty edifice of America is being reared.

THE ARCHITECTS OF CONCORD

It was a time of expectation. Every sensitive spirit felt the quiver of impending change. The industrial revolution was beginning, pregnant with promise, disquieting in its slum-sweatshop-body-breaking fulfillment. The train of political revolutions was continuing. Men from the Atlantic seaboard and European immigrants were pouring into the West. All eyes were on America as that new and virgin land where life might be refashioned after man's dreams. "It is a land of desire for all those who are weary of the historical lumber-room of old Europe." . . . So wrote Hegel, for even he in the stuffy Prussia he was straining to idealize, stirred uneasily with the Utopian dream.

As for the architects of Concord, they carried projects in their vest pockets and produced fresh blueprints daily for the building of the promised land. "It is a country of beginnings," Rivera quotes from Emerson, "of projects, of vast designs and expectations. It has no past: all has an onward and prospective look." And from Thoreau: "All things invite this earth's inhabitants to rear their lives to an unheard of height, and meet the expectation of the land."

Calvinism, with its universal damnation, grim fruit of the universal hell that life had been in Europe for the century or two in which feudalism was dying and capitalism powerless to be born, gave way to Universalism and Unitarianism, with their optimistic belief in the essential goodness of humanity and the possibility of universal salvation, spiritual reflections of the apparent possibilities on the frontier for material success and happiness for all.

The material foundations of the structure were concealed in the mystic, rose-tinted clouds of transcendental philosophy, and with Utopianism and Transcendentalism, a host of other "isms"—individualism and perfectionism, vegetarianism and dress reform, bloomers and graham bread, "aspiring vegetables" and woman's rights, abolitionism and universal education, prison reform and a new attitude towards debtors and the insane, mesmerism and phrenology, temperance and "loco-focoism"—generous dreams and whimsical crotchets inextricably intermingled in the yeasty, frothy, heady drink brewing in the America of the '30's and '40's. Rivera has selected three of the noblest of the dreamers, Thoreau, Emerson, and Margaret Fuller, and in their book, he has put excerpts expressive of their love of freedom, their pathetic faith in individualism, their refusal to compromise with slavery, their Utopian dreams. A few listen to them, and a few covered wagons take up the trail to Utopia. The trail is painted in unreal pale pinks and blues; Utopia is a replica of the Parthenon, cold and classic and out of place in the America of rising factory towns and rough frontier.

THE DREAM AND THE REALITY

The architecture of Utopia, on closer inspection, turns out to be an echo of the National Bank, and the skyline of Utopia blends into the skyline of the 1840 mill-town Lowell, which in turn runs into the skyline of the West. For the expansive dreams of the individualism-worshipping Emerson and Thoreau have served but to give a transcendental glow to the filibustering dreams of land expansion of the Polks and the Austins and the Houstons, and the dreams of wealth expansion of the Hamiltons and Astors. And once the free land of the West has disappeared and the small enterprise has been dispossessed by the huge banking house and the trust, then the equalitarianism and individualism of the Concord dreamers withers away, for it has lost its economic roots.

THE FATE OF FRONTIER DEMOCRACY

So too the frontier dream of democracy, symbolized in the figure of Andrew Jackson, was utilized by the very forces behind the bank, the tariff, and the money power, to strengthen the hold of rising capitalism upon America. The first of that long series of presidential nonentities, William Henry Harrison, was trotted out; his elegant mansion became a log cabin; democracy was reduced to the democratic dispensation of hard cider; a little Indian skirmish elevated into the decisive battle of Tippecanoe; Jackson's attempt to clean out the "aristocrats" from the permanent office-holding bureaucracy degenerated into the spoils system; and the party platform and party bosses hidden behind a ballyhoo of democracy, log cabins, hard cider and Indian fighting, converted the Jefferson-Jackson dream of a petty-bourgeois democracy into democratic trappings for the future role of big business.

THE DREAM OF THE INVENTOR

The panel is full of machinery: the sewing machine that was to lighten labor in the home, but brought the sweatshop; the telegraph that was to transmit the liberating thoughts of men, but served to transmit dispatches in the Mexican War; the railroad and steamboat that were to transport men and things, and were immediately utilized for soldiers and munitions; the rifles supporting Polk's map and the Colt's revolver invented just in time for use in the Mexican War; the factories that were to produce leisure and plenty but produced artificial poverty amidst choking "surplus" and leisure in the grisly form of unemployment.

Brigham Young dreamed of organizing a cooperative Zion, but the elders of Zion are today the directors of sugar mills, copper and silver mines, railroads and other huge corporations, and have political, social, religious, and economic control over a whole region.

America before 1850 was a land of boundless energy; of generous enthusiasms; of vague and noble dreams. But dreams, enthusiasms, and boundless energy were in the end canalized into serving the main stream of American development, the stream being charted by Hamilton, deepened by the Astors, widened by Polk—the mighty river of American capitalist development.

PANEL V THE CONFLICT OVER SLAVERY

THE background of Panel V is formed by the Mexican War and the discovery of gold in California. Between the heads of Generals Zachary Taylor and Winfield Scott are Mexican battle scenes. The troops that were raised to challenge England—"Fifty-four forty or fight"—were turned against Mexico. It was much easier, and more profitable. Besides, Mexican land was southern land, slavery land; and Mexico had abolished slavery! Southern expansionists under the leadership of Calhoun forced annexation of Texas and war with Mexico. The spread of slavery seemed assured.

THE BLOODY HAND

The land seized from Mexico was shown in the preceding panel covered by the hand of President Polk. Here the map is still visible and the hand has left a bloody imprint on the conquered territory. To Mexico it was the bloody hand of unrighteous aggression. To America it proved to be the bloody hand of civil war.

GOLD

The central background is glowing with the purple hills and sunlit waters of the Golden Gate, and at the right, scenes of placer mining in the Sierras dominated by the figure of James W. Marshall holding in his hand a shining golden nugget.

Fatal unity of opposites! Inevitable historical polarity! The drive of the Southern slave holders for the extension of slave territory brought with it the simultaneous and more rapid expansion of Northern wealth and power. California lay largely south of the Mason and Dixon line, but the gold rush was no rush of slave owners and cotton planters. The land wrested from Mexico was in part cotton land and tobacco land. But it was much more copper, lead, and oil land, silver and gold land. The mineral wealth seized from Mexico at the instance of the slavocracy was destined to reinforce its mortal enemy, industrial capitalism, to make American capitalism the richest in the world. The gold rush to the coast was to people the West with a population of small farmers and homesteaders. The transcontinental railroads were to cut the cord that bound West and South and to tie up inextricably the West with the North. The settling of the Pacific Coast was some day to produce the war with Spain, the annexation of the Philippines, the entrance of the United States into the Pacific, the Panama Canal, the development of American capitalism into the imperialist capitalism of a world power.

THE IRREPRESSIBLE CONFLICT

The Mexican War was intended by Calhoun and his followers to safeguard slavery forever. Yet, no sooner did it begin than the conflict over slavery flared up afresh. How often had it been "settled"! But the conflict was irrepressible. It was a conflict between two opposing and expanding social systems. The slave system demanded wide stretches of naturally fertile soil, because its primitive character rapidly exhausted the older lands. These became slave-breeding regions and clamored for fresh markets for their "peculiar product." Industrial capitalism was no less an expanding system. Both attempted to occupy the West. Both wrestled for control of the national government and its policies. The expansion of America brought with it the expansion of this fatal inner antagonism. But with the victory of the South in forcing the Mexican War (not without the aid of Northerners who had invested in Texas bonds), Northern anti-slavery sentiment was at last aroused in deadly earnest. From then on, the struggle against slavery overshadowed all other issues, enlisted all the generous idealism that had in the previous decade attached to so many causes, and became a mighty torrent destined to overwhelm the slaveholding system.

CALIFORNIA
GOLD REGION DIRECT
JOSEPHINE
10th November Best
RODNEY FRENCH
RUN away
JOE
REWARD
CHINESE BANK
AUCTION THIS DAY
Calhoun
UNCLE TOM'S CABIN
Down WITH THIS ACCURSED SYSTEM OF SLAVERY
affirm as a fundamental principle that
the creator of wealth is entitled
to all it creates.....
enlightened mind a scene of civil war
more sickening than 100 years of

In the '30's and '40's every thinker and dreamer in the North and West was something of a Utopian socialist, and when Robert Owen came to America, the Congress of the United States invited him to appear before them and tell them how they might abolish capitalism! In the '50's every great name in letters and thought is more or less intimately connected with the anti-slavery struggle.

The names of those who were in turn linked up with both movements read like an honor role of America's great men of the time: Emerson, Thoreau, Hawthorne, Greeley, Dana, Lowell, Parker, Godwin, Whittier, Ripley, Alcott, Clarke, Brownson, the Channings, Bryant, Margaret Fuller, to mention only a few of them.

OPPONENTS OF THE WAR

Rivera has filled middle and foreground of this panel with slaves and slave drivers and the outstanding opponents, as well as the outstanding apologist for slavery. Thoreau has gotten himself into jail for his uncompromising opposition to the Mexican War and extension of slavery. If the same procedure had been employed as was used during the World War, all of New England's thinkers and leaders would have been in jail with him. Lowell openly advocated resistance to the war in his *Bigelow Papers*. Whittier's verses rang with indignation and summons to resistance. The Massachusetts legislature denounced the "unconstitutional" war "for the dismemberment of Mexico" and "the triple object of extending slavery, of strengthening the Slave Power, and of obtaining the control of the Free States." United States senators openly expressed their sympathy with Mexico, prayed for Mexican victory, and hoped that the defenders of Mexico would welcome our soldiers "to hospitable graves."

But in those days a more progressive America did not dream of punishing the utterance of opinion, and Thoreau alone landed in jail, not for his burning words but for refusing to pay his poll tax to an "iniquitous government"! The spirit of the times is well illustrated in the famous anecdote of the visit of Emerson to Thoreau in his cell, when Emerson asked: "Henry, what are you doing in there?" and Thoreau replied, "Waldo, what are you doing out there?" This spirit has been expressed by Rivera's reproduction of Thoreau's burning words, written in jail: "The prison is the only home in a slave state in which a free man can abide with honor."

CALHOUN, SLAVERY'S GREATEST DEFENDER

As representative of the apologists for slavery, Rivera has selected John C. Calhoun, one of the most intelligent statesmen that America produced during the 19th Century. In senatorial polemic, Calhoun was invincible, for he raised issues to which conservative, capitalist-minded Northern politicians could find no answer. "There has never yet existed a wealthy and civilized society in which one portion of the community did not live on the labor of the other," he told the defenders of Northern capitalism. His unflinching realism exposed their own hypocritical attacks upon slavery as the only form of exploitation of man by man. "The person who works for wages is exploited more severely than the chattel laborer," he told them. What, he asked, did Northern capitalism do with its "wage slaves" when it did not happen to need them? Left them on the street to starve. When old and infirm? Let them starve. How did it treat the children of "wage-slaves"? Let them starve. But the Southern slave-owner had at least a property-holder's interest in conserving a valuable animal. He took care of the children of his slaves when they were not yet old enough to work. He took care of his slaves when ill, when unemployed, when old and infirm. What did the wage-slaves of the North get in return for their labor? Food, clothing, shelter, *when* and *if* their labor was needed. What did the chattel slaves of the South get in return for their labor? Food, clothing, and shelter from birth to death.

Or he bade them compare the life of the leisure class, North and

South. The purpose of slavery in all its forms, he declared, was the creation of a leisure class who might develop culture. He summoned up the resources of academic learning to remind his opponents that the greatest culture so far produced, the culture of ancient Greece, had rested on the basis of chattel slavery. But the North? The North had no leisure class worthy of the name. Its wealthy were too occupied with money-grubbing; they spent their time in the counting house and the market place. The South sent gentlemen of the first families to the Senate; the North sent lawyers. The North produced neither gallantry nor chivalry, neither gentlemen nor statesmen. The North had slavery without the fruits of slavery, without a culture worthy of the name.

Finally, argued Calhoun, the Northern system implied cities and slums, vice and disease, and above all class conflict. "It is impossible with us that the conflict can take place between labor and capital, which makes it so difficult to establish and maintain free institutions in all wealthy and highly civilized nations. . . ."

In a word, Calhoun laid bare the exploitative roots, the class domination, involved in both systems. And to this, the Northern statesmen who regarded capitalist exploitation as the very summit of human freedom, had no answer.

Only the Utopian socialists, the Ripleys, Danas, Greeleys, Parkers, Brownsons, Brisbanes, could answer, and the Utopians were not in the Senate. Even the abolitionists, with rare exceptions, did not see beyond wage-slavery as the equivalent of absolute freedom.

SLAVE REVOLT

One of Calhoun's arguments, at least, was given decisive refutation by slave rebellions, by physical-force abolitionists, by the Civil War. These annihilated his contention that the slave-system was immune from class struggle.

Orthodox American historians are strangely silent about the thirty-odd Negro rebellions in American history, among them Cato's rebellion in 1740, Gabriel's Insurrection, 1800, Denmark Vesey's rebellion, 1822, and the movement led by Nat Turner in 1831, which alone receives meager mention in the text books, perhaps because it was the last great revolt and occurred at a time when the Abolitionist movement had begun, so that it was hailed among the whites.

As representative leaders of slave revolts, Rivera has painted, opposite Calhoun, the figures of Nat Turner and John Brown. Below them is the face of the great Negro abolitionist, himself an escaped slave, Frederick Douglass. He was no pacifist like Garrison, who was willing to see slavery continue in the South provided only it was separated from the North. Nor did Douglass content himself with denouncing Southern slavery. He fought unceasingly against Northern discrimination and Jim Crowism. An advocate of armed struggle like John Brown, he was more of a realist and sought to dissuade him from the desperate venture at Harper's Ferry. He was undoubtedly one of the greatest of the abolitionists, but again the history books are mainly silent, for his face was black!

Another black-skinned abolitionist whom the academic historians ignore is Sojourner Truth. She is painted in the center of the foreground next to the great anti-slavery novelist, Harriet Beecher Stowe. Sojourner Truth was also an escaped slave, illiterate, but with a vast native intelligence and powers of oratory that worsted many Northern preachers and politicians in debates on abolition and feminism, for she was a champion of both.

Between Frederick Douglass and Harriet Beecher Stowe stand the figures of William Lloyd Garrison (with glasses) and of Wendell Phillips (holding a scroll) . Garrison is there as the tireless and uncompromising agitator, as the flaming conscience that would not be put out. The appearance of his *Liberator* in 1831 initiated the modern abolitionist movement. His stirring words in the first number of that journal can still serve as text for all fighters for freedom:

*"I will be as harsh as truth, and as uncompromising as justice. . . .
I am in earnest—I will not equivocate—I will not excuse—
I will not retreat a single inch—AND I WILL BE HEARD."*

WENDELL PHILLIPS

But the outstanding place among the abolitionists Rivera has properly given to the leaders of slave revolts, Nat Turner and John Brown, and to the most far-seeing of all the abolitionists, Wendell Phillips. Of a distinguished Boston family (his father was Boston's first mayor and his ancestry Puritan and revolutionary), he abandoned a hopeful career at the age of 24 to join the Anti-slavery Society, then being formed by Garrison, and to devote his entire life to anti-slavery agitation and social reform. He espoused woman suffrage, prison reform, temperance, Irish freedom, Polish freedom, Haitian freedom, the cause of the workingman. He unhesitatingly urged slave rebellion, civil war, and resistance to the Fugitive Slave Act. His eloquent tongue was never enlisted in an ignoble cause, never silent in a worthy one. And almost alone of all the active abolitionists, he had the vision to see that the abolition of slavery was but the abolition of a semi-feudal, anachronistic form of exploitation, in favor of the capitalist form. When the Civil War ended, the other abolitionists were silent: there was nothing more to do! But ere the echo of the guns of Civil War had died away, November 2, 1865, found Phillips once more in Faneuil Hall supporting the workingman's struggle for an eight-hour day. And in 1871 he drafted the platform and made the keynote speech of the Labor-Reform Convention at Worcester and ran for Governor on the labor ticket.

As he had devoted his earlier life to abolition, so the last thirteen years of his life he devoted to labor's cause. In 1881, in one of his last public appearances before his death, he chose in the Phi Beta Kappa centennial oration before Harvard University to hail the Russian

Nihilists in the struggle against Czarism, as earlier he had hailed the Paris Commune in 1871, and had chosen as the theme for his Phi Beta Kappa address at Yale in 1857, "The Republican Scholar of Necessity an Agitator."

"LIBERAL" historians, whose main stock in trade is the conviction that all progress takes place at a snail's pace and that "force never accomplished anything," declare that "the Civil War was unnecessary" and "slavery was doomed anyhow." This owl-like "wisdom" which takes flight only after the day is done, is refuted by the decades of conflict which preceded and the decades of conflict which followed the Civil War. What was secession, if not an evidence that the slave-owning class, as all privileged classes throughout history, was determined that it would not give up its privileges without a fight? And what was the Ku Klux Klan if not an effort to re-establish by force as many features of slavery as possible? For almost half a century the struggle between the two rival social systems was the axis around which turned the whole domestic and foreign history of America.

JOHN BROWN

Not Abraham Lincoln, but John Brown is Rivera's hero and martyr of the Civil War. In the preceding panel, John Brown's figure is plastically the outstanding one. Here it is to be found twice, in both lower and upper foreground, occupying the whole "beginning" of the picture.

The lower section is set off by a wooden frame on which are painted the words from Marx's *Capital:* "Labor with a white skin cannot emancipate itself where labor with a black skin is branded." Brown is seen leading his heroic raid at Harper's Ferry, based on the belief "that upon the first intimation of a plan formed for the liberation of slaves, they would immediately rise all over the Southern States."

With a little band of 22 men, 17 whites and 5 Negroes, John Brown attacked and captured the arsenal at Harper's Ferry and freed and armed many slaves. The attack was no sudden impulse, but carefully planned and preceded by years of discussion and preparation. A previous raid in Missouri had resulted in the liberation of great numbers of slaves and their escape to Canada. This time the raid was again successful, but John Brown did not retreat. He had prepared a Constitution for a Free Republic which was to maintain itself by guerrilla warfare in the Appalachian Mountains, and spread through slave insurrections throughout the South. He had Parker prepare an address to the officers and soldiers of the United States army. But he miscalculated the slowness with which slave revolts would spread in the South, underestimated the speed with which telegraph, railway, and frantic Virginian and National governments (both pro-slavery) would react against him, overlooked the difference between the Missouri-Kansas border and the vicinity of the National capital, and forgot that against Southern pro-slavery troops (under the command of Col. Robert E. Lee!) propaganda for freedom would be of little avail.

Three days he held the arsenal. Ten of his heroic little band were killed, including two of his own sons (shown flanking him in the picture), seven were captured and hanged, and five escaped into the hills and made their way by the underground railway to Canada. John Brown was brutally wounded by an officer's sabre and two bayonet thrusts, after being captured! And while still suffering from his wounds he was hastily and fearfully "tried," denied opportunity to send for Northern counsel, assigned two Southern pro-slavery lawyers, refused facilities for subpoenaing witnesses, and convicted within three days, of "treason, and conspiring and advising with slaves and other rebels, and murder in the first degree." He was captured by an officer, convicted by a court, and executed under orders of a governor and official apparatus, who were already conspiring their own treason and rebellion under the banner, not of freedom, but of slavery! Within a month he was hanged, lest his contagious example spread. The advice he had given the resisters of the fugitive slave law, he followed himself:

"Be hanged, if you must, but tell no tales out of school." Neither Parker, nor Gerrit Smith, nor any of the other abolitionists who aided him, was implicated.

His example in the death cell was even more potent than in the arsenal. He refused to plead insanity, or ask for mercy. To his wife he wrote, "Tell them their father died without a single regret for the course he has pursued. . . ." His last written words handed to a guard on the morning of his execution, were:

"I, John Brown, am now quite certain *that the crimes of this* guilty land *will never be purged away but with* blood. *I had, as I now think vainly, flattered myself that without very much bloodshed it might be done."*

So he marched to his death, proudly, defiantly, knowing that his death was but the continuation of his life, his last and greatest service to the anti-slavery cause. "I am worth inconceivably more to *hang,*" he proclaimed, "than for any other purpose."

Dying for the cause of freedom, he shamed others into living for it. "These men," was Thoreau's way of putting it, "in teaching us how to die, have at the same time taught us how to live."

North and South, the nation stirred uneasily. Slave revolts broke out in Missouri. Slaves showed increased restlessness everywhere. Free Negroes were hastily deported from the big cities. Huge funeral demonstrations were held throughout the North and West and even in Europe. Victor Hugo addressed America in these terms:

"John Brown . . . is to be hanged today . . . his hangman (we shudder to think it and say it!) is the whole American Republic. . . . It will deal the Union a concealed wound which will sunder the states."

And the poet Stedman chanted prophetically:

"And Old Brown
Ossawattomie Brown,
May trouble you more than ever when
you've nailed his coffin down!"

His epitaph was written with bayonets and punctuated with cannon and the ground tone of his funeral hymn was the sound of tramping feet as hundreds of thousands marched to war singing:

> *"John Brown's body lies a-mouldering in the grave,*
> *But his soul goes marching on."*

The raid of John Brown initiated the anti-slavery struggle in the Civil War as the raid on Fort Sumter initiated the pro-slavery struggle. That is Rivera's reason for making John Brown's raid the "cornerstone" and his hanging the "starting point" of the Civil War.

ABRAHAM LINCOLN

Rivera's Lincoln is a truer portrait than either ikon-making or ikon-breaking historians have painted. The one set have seized upon his humble origin, have utilized the stand-behind-the-president war atmosphere, and the halo of martyrdom, to make of him the planner and initiator of the struggle against slavery, the friend of the Negro people, the "Great Emancipator." The "debunkers" have seized upon his inconsistencies, his vacillations and compromises, his schemings for political advancement, his evasions that won him a presidential nomination over the consistent abolitionist founders and leaders of his party when a dark-horse vote-getter was needed, and have sought to reduce him to the stature of a "peanut politician." Neither group has portrayed the true Lincoln.

LINCOLN AND THE NEGRO

Lincoln was by no means an abolitionist. He repeatedly attacked the abolitionists as trouble-makers, as tending "rather to increase slavery's evils." He was not for full economic, political, and social equality for the Negro race. In Illinois, when running for the Legislature, he had declared for the extension of the right of suffrage to all whites, male and female, but made no mention of free Negroes. In

ON THE FIRST DAY OF JANUARY IN THE YEAR OF OUR LORD ONE THOUSAND EIGHT HUNDRED AND SIXTY-THREE, ALL PERSONS HELD AS SLAVES WITHIN ANY STATE, THE PEOPLE WHEREOF SHALL THEN BE IN REBELLION AGAINST THE UNITED STATES, SHALL BE THEN, THENCEFORWARD AND FOREVER FREE.
LINCOLN
SKIN CANNOT EMANCIPATE ITSELF WHERE LABOR WITH A BLACK SKIN IS BRANDED _ KARL MARX

1854, he asked: "Free them, and make them politically and socially our equals? My own feelings will not admit of this. . . . We cannot make them equals." For years he gave half-hearted support to the fugitive slave laws, and even accepted as attorney the case of a slave-owner suing in Illinois for the recapture of fugitive slaves. Clearly he was no crusader, no vanguard leader, in the long struggle to arouse the conscience of the North and West against slavery and for the extension of the "rights of man" to the Negro. Only when his Whig party, whose support of bank and tariff and internal improvements he heartily endorsed, was in decay, and when Whig and Democratic parties alike were splitting wide open on the slavery question, did Lincoln (in 1856) go over to a moderate Republicanism. Wendell Phillips hailed his election to the presidency in these terms:

"Not an Abolitionist, hardly an antislavery man, Mr. Lincoln consents to represent an antislavery idea. A pawn on the political chessboard, his value is in his position. . . . Lincoln is in place, *Garrison in* power."

During the Civil War, he gradually developed in stature and went from "place" to "power." But in his conduct of the war, his temperamental caution and reservations on Negro equality were reinforced by the pressure of the Border States and the awkward predicament of early Northern defeats. The Radical Republicans had expected that once war was declared the North would wage it by revolutionary means, that is, proclaim the emancipation of the slaves, enlist Negro soldiers, and encourage slave revolts, thus utilizing the inherent weakness in the Southern social structure to bring the war to a speedy conclusion. Greeley, Stevens, Fremont, Phillips, and the radical abolitionists generally, were disappointed and indignant.

"Our statesmen do not seem to know how to touch the hearts of freemen and rouse them to battle. No sound of universal liberty has gone forth from the Capitol. Our generals have a sword in one hand and shackles in the other. Let it be known that this government is

fighting to carry out the great principles of the Declaration of Independence and the blood of every freeman would boil with enthusiasm and his nerves be strengthened for the holy warfare. Give him the sword in one hand and the book of freedom in the other, and he will soon sweep despotism from every corner of this continent."

So spoke Thaddeus Stevens. Greeley wrote, in an open letter to Lincoln:

"Future generations will with difficulty realize that there could have been hesitation on this point." And Marx, who was anxiously following the Civil War and rallying support for the North among the workers of England and the European continent, wrote to Engels:

"Lincoln's acts have all the appearance of the pettifogging stipulation clauses which an attorney presents to his opponent."

But in the next line, Marx added, and this is a lesson to the "debunking" school of historians: "This does not interfere with their historical content. . . ."

It was this rounded verdict of Marx that Rivera had in mind in portraying his figure of Lincoln. It is in the face that contemplates with half-comprehending eyes the hanging body of John Brown. It is in the irony that portrays Lincoln confronting the hanging figure with the Emancipation Proclamation which the living drafted but the dead began. It is in the double-columned inscription in Lincoln's hands—on the right:

"I have no purpose to introduce political and social equality between the white and the black race. . . . I would save the Union. . . . If I could save the Union without freeing any slaves I would do it; if I could save it by freeing all I would do it; if I could do it by freeing some and leaving others alone, I would also do that. . . ."

And on the left, the evidence that Lincoln's "pettifogging stipulations" and subjective hesitations could not hinder nor interfere with his objective historical role:

"On the first day of January in the year of our Lord one thousand

eight hundred and sixty-three, all persons held as slaves within any State, the people whereof shall then be in rebellion against the United States, shall be then, thenceforward and forever free."

J. P. MORGAN, THE FIRST

How far the Civil War was to play a consistently progressive role was to be determined, not merely by Congress, with its majority of Radical Republicans, nor by the President with his limited views on the rights of Negroes, nor by the actual tactics pursued in the conduct of the military phases of the Civil War. All of these were important, but decisive was the differentiation of classes and programs in the victorious Northern camp after the success of their united effort. The political form in which this conflict took place is the struggle between Presidents Lincoln and Johnson on the one hand, and Congress on the other, over Reconstruction, and the factional controversy between conservatives and radicals for control of the Republican Party. The outcome of this controversy was favorable to the conservatives, largely because the War, besides its progressive features (the preservation of economic unity and the destruction of chattel slavery and pre-capitalist economy), brought in its train an enormous strengthening of bankers and industrialists, of railroad "builders" and speculators, who in turn converted the multi-class Republican Party where agrarians and industrialists were disputing for power, into an instrument of Northern, i.e. national, capitalism. J. P. Morgan the First is selected here to represent that aspect of the Civil War.

FOUNDATIONS OF THE MORGAN FORTUNE

Morgan's father, Junius S. Morgan, was already wealthy as a partner in George Peabody and Company, Civil War bankers. One of J. P. Morgan's first ascertainable business transactions on his own was the purchase, through an agent, of 5,000 old rifles auctioned off by the Government as junk since it was feared that they would explode in the hands of the soldiers if they were used. Morgan's agent then telegraphed General Frémont in St. Louis offering 5,000 new carbines "in perfect condition" at $22 a rifle! All this was made a matter of Congressional and legal record, but Morgan sued and got his money from the Courts! This shabby deal, and his speculation in gold later in the war, laid the foundation of the personally "earned" fortune of the first J. P. Morgan. Out of the Civil War, its national banking act, its railroad grants, its speculation and profiteering, grew the great fortunes of the money kings who are the rulers of America today.

The most imposing figure of them all is J. P. Morgan; Rivera has painted him in all his "magnificence" as the representative of his tribe, with his right hand on his money bag (echoed by the lines of his bulbous nose) surrounded by his rifles, while in the background we see the rifles exploding into the faces of Northern soldiers. His left hand reaches into the next panel where it subsidizes and supports reaction in the Reconstruction period. His influence and his dynastic heirs dominate America and much of the world today.

THE Radical Republicans were the continuators of the work of the Abolitionists. The anti-slavery vanguard arose and developed in isolation from the class whose interests they represented, and from the masses as a whole. Their early fate was ridicule and even savage persecution by those who were later to follow them. And their fate today is virtual oblivion.

The early 1930's marked the 100th anniversary of the founding of various local and national anti-slavery societies, but a nation which makes official centennials of every insignificant triviality or nonentity, had no word to say concerning these heroes.

As for the Radical Republicans, whose fate it was, after leading the nation through the Civil War and early Reconstruction, again to be abandoned by the class they represented, and to have their efforts for a radical solution of the Negro problem end in failure—they have gone down in official history as "vengeful and venomous," as "hateful fanatics," as men "hard and unforgiving and bitter," as "conspirators and thieves," and even as "rats, bats and snakes." It is these Radicals, Wade (lower right) and Stevens (holding the scroll) and Sumner (behind Stevens), that Rivera has selected to be the "heroes" of his Reconstruction panel, the protagonists of the great conflict between progress and reaction that marked the final stage of the Civil War. The victorious force that opposed them is represented by the hand of Morgan, by the Grand Imperial Wizard in mask and full regalia, by the fiery cross and lynching pyre, the night riders spreading terror, and the Konklave of the Ku Klux Klan.

The Civil War and Reconstruction period constitute two stages of what was essentially a single bourgeois revolution. The first stage was the defeat of the armed counter-revolution, and the second, the attempt

A great city is that which
where the slave ceases and
the master of the slaves ceases
where the populace rises at once
against the never-ending auda-
-city of elected persons...
WALT WHITMAN
It is a radical revolution intended to remodel our institutions. It is intended to work a radical reorganization in Southern institutions, habits and manners...
The foundations of their
institutions must be broken up
and relaid, or all our blood and
treasure have been spent in vain...

to draw all the historically necessary consequences, economic, political, and social, from the victory of progressive capitalism over pre-capitalist conditions and a pre-capitalist ruling class. In spite of highly specific differences, the aims of the revolutionary party were basically those of the classic bourgeois-democratic revolution: the consolidation of national political and economic unity (the defeat of secession and of "States Rights"), the thorough eradication of all pre-capitalist economic forms (abolition of slavery and the plantation system), the destruction of the political power of the landed aristocracy (disfranchisement of the former slaveowners and rebels and smashing of the economic basis of their political power), the advance of democracy (the enfranchisement of the Negroes and poor whites in the South), the agrarian revolution (the Radical plan of confiscating the lands of the former slave-owners for distribution among the emancipated slaves), the establishment of capitalist-wage-labor relations, etc.

THE RADICALS

The men of the Reconstruction were thoroughly conscious of this role which the historians have so completely forgotten. Even the moderate Carl Schurz wrote in his report to President Johnson in 1865 after a tour of the South:

"The general government of the republic has, by proclaiming the emancipation of the slaves, commenced a great social revolution in the south, but has, as yet, not completed it."

Thaddeus Stevens, the greatest of the Radical leaders, proclaimed the intentions of his group in unequivocal words, some of which Rivera has painted on the scroll in his hands:

"It is a radical revolution intended to remodel our institutions. It is intended to work a radical reorganization in Southern institutions, habits and manners. . . . The foundations . . . must be broken up and relaid, or all our blood and treasure have been spent in vain. . . ."

Two paths and two outcomes are possible in every bourgeois revolution: the radical (Jacobin) and the conservative (Girondin). Charles Sumner, who was in the Senate from 1851 until his death in 1874 and from first to last faithfully championed the cause of Negro freedom and rights, Benjamin Wade, the great agrarian radical who was President of the Senate and in line for the presidency if Johnson's impeachment had gone through, and Thad Stevens, the great leader of the House of Representatives, these are the "Jacobins" whom Rivera has portrayed. With them he has somewhat incorrectly placed the poet whom he considers not only America's greatest, but the greatest that the 19th century produced, Walt Whitman. Whitman's record on the slavery question is by no means that of the Radicals, and his great fire was dying down by the time the Civil War had ended. He more properly belongs with Emerson, Margaret Fuller, and Thoreau—in our opinion, the only error in historical judgment that Rivera has made in his stirring and penetrating portrayal of our history.

A TIME OF HESITATION

At first the radical course had the upper hand and it seemed as if it would triumph. The Southern ruling class had too soon showed its hand by passing the brutal "Black Codes" in the legislatures of the provisional governments set up in 1865. The theory of these ordinances was that the Negro, though nominally free, required the economic and political "guardianship" of the former master; the practice was a foreshadowing of the new forms of subjection which the South has since elaborated. Harsh vagrancy laws made unemployment a crime, and the newly freed slaves, landless and homeless, were all unemployed. Heavy fines for vagrancy were to be "worked off" in the custody of whoever paid the fine. This was supplemented by a system of "apprenticeship." Children at the age of two might become apprentices! Some states put a head tax on all Negroes (and only on Negroes!), which, if unpaid—and what ex-slave could pay it?—was "prima facie evidence of vagrancy." It was made a crime to carry a knife or firearm, a crime to enter a white church, railroad car, or public assemblage of white persons, a crime for Negroes to assemble.

This it was that caused even such moderates as Carl Schurz and General Grant, virtually every Northern investigator sent into the South in 1865, to urge Lincoln and Johnson to abandon the conservative course they were advocating. This course would have permitted the states to re-enter the Union after acknowledging the formal freedom of the Negro, and the Southern ruling class to reconstitute its old regime under new legal forms.

The Radicals advocated military protection for the Negroes, smashing of the power of the old Southern ruling class by confiscating their large estates, giving an economic foundation to the juridical freedom of the ex-slaves by distributing the rebel estates to them. "Forty acres of land and a hut," declared Stevens, "would be more valuable to the freedman than the immediate right to vote."

REACTION

The Radicals had a big majority in Congress. For a while they overwhelmed the resistance of the Southern ruling class; upset the executive dictatorship of Lincoln who was putting through his plan by executive decree; overrode the vetoes of Johnson; and when he sought to continue the presidential dictatorship, planned to impeach him.

But the Civil War, like every bourgeois revolution, involved two contradictory though inseparable historical motives. As a progressive and revolutionary class, supported, even driven, by the petty bourgeoisie and proletariat, the bourgeoisie proceeds ruthlessly to destroy all pre-capitalist forms, to clear the way for bourgeois democracy and equality before the law. As a capitalist class, it uses its newly won state power as a lever to stimulate the accumulation of capital, and the expansion of its mode of production. In proportion as it is victorious it begins to demand a halt to the revolution, to shrink in terror from the popular forces it has unleashed, and to throw itself into the arms of its former opponent, now harmless as a contender but useful as an ally for "law and order."

For the Northern capitalist class, already developed and powerful because of the historical "lateness" of its struggle, the second motive was dominant from the beginning, and the war-time protective tariff, the banking act of 1863, the railway land grants which handed out empires, the war speculation and profiteering, enormously strengthened the forces of big capital and laid the foundations of its subsequent power. This class soon overthrew the petty-bourgeois, Western farmer leadership in the Republican Party, liquidated radicalism except for campaign oratory ("the bloody shirt"), reduced Reconstruction more and more to a question of retaining its hold on the Federal government, and transformed the Republican party into a party of big business.

While Benjamin Wade, the president of the Senate, was declaring: "After the abolition of slavery, a radical change in the relations of capital and of property in land is next upon the order of the day," while Butler and Stevens were preparing the impeachment of Johnson (which, by a last minute switch of one vote, just failed of putting Wade into the presidency), Henry Cooke of the banking firm of Jay Cooke and Company, was writing:

"You know how I have felt for a long time, in regard to the course of the ultra-infidelic radicals like Wade, Sumner, Stevens, et id omne genus. They were dragging the Republican party into all sorts of isms and extremes. Their policy was one of bitterness, hate, and wild agrarianism. These reckless demagogues have had their day and the time has come for wiser counsel. With Wade uttering agrarian doctrines in Kansas and fanning the flames of vulgar prejudices, trying to array labor against capital and pandering to the basest passions; with Butler urging wholesale conscription throughout the South and whole-

sale repudiation throughout the North . . . ; with Stevens . . . advocating the idea of a flood of irredeemable paper money . . . ; with Pomeroy and Wade and Sprague and a host of others clamoring for the unsexing of woman and putting a ballot in her hand . . . what wonder is it that the accumulated load was too heavy for any party to carry . . . ?"

This reaction Rivera indicates by showing the tops of three "cylinder hats" visible behind the Ku Klux Klan, by portraying Morgan's hand reaching over from the preceding panel with financial aid for Southern reaction, by his background of coolie labor constructing the transcontinental railway, by the chain-gangs of blacks and whites working under armed overseers, by the strikers being driven back to work by mounted police, by the night-riders spreading terror and reaction, by the hanging and burning Negroes who took too seriously the brief dream of freedom and equality.

PANEL VIII THE LABOR MOVEMENT

PANEL VIII marks the end of one wall of the hall of the New Workers' School in which the murals are housed. It also marks the end of one phase of American history and the prelude to the next. It introduces a change in subject matter, a change in mood and treatment, a shift in "center of gravity."

The defeat of the Southern plantation aristocracy, followed by the defeat of agrarian and petty bourgeois radicalism, has left capitalist industrialism in triumphant possession of the field. No longer is the theory of aristocracy openly advanced. But democracy, fast losing its frontier equalitarianism and earlier militancy, has also ceased to be a living force. The Fourth of July is piously dedicated to Jefferson, or to flags and fireworks, Election day is still ushered in with incantations in the name of Jackson and Lincoln, but the other 363 days of the year are sacred to Alexander Hamilton. As the petty bourgeoisie has yielded to the great, the forms of bourgeois democracy have revealed themselves as but the outer wrappings of plutocracy. Hamilton's dream of the rule of the rich and the well-born has narrowed down to the rule of the rich.

With the disappearance of the frontier and the triumph of big business, Western agrarianism enters into the stage of a retreating and losing fight. Class lines lose their singular American fluidity and America slowly begins to rediscover, in its modern Marxian or scientific form, the class struggle and class structure of society which formed the foundation of the political thinking of Madison and Hamilton. Henceforward, the main stream of American history is clearly the history of American capitalism, and its main opponent is no longer agrarianism, but labor. The history of America as the "history of class struggles" has taken on a new simplicity—and a new intensity.

MASS-MEETING
HAYMARKET
What do you think of the Workers of the United
States? This first explosion against the associa-
ted oligarchy of capital will naturally again
be suppressed, but can well form the point of origin for the constitution of an earnest workers'
party. The policy of the new president will make
the Negroes, and the great expropriations of land
will make the already dissatisfied farmers of
the West, into allies of
the workers.
KARL
MARX
FIRST INTERNATIONAL

The triumph of the capitalist class over all intermediate classes has brought it face to face with its indispensable servant and mortal enemy, the working class. Not that a modern working class movement has sprung fully conscious, fully armed, from the forehead of Marx. The working class does not attain to consciousness that way. On the contrary, there is a confusion of many voices, a conflict of many creeds, a compound of many hard-dying illusions.

Here is Johann Most (lower left) calling the workers in words of fire, to anarchy. Here is Henry George (above Most) summoning them to battle in the name of a war on monopoly in land. Here is Terence V. Powderly, Grand Master Workman of the Knights of Labor, urging cooperation, arbitration, organization in ritualistic secret societies. Samuel Gompers should be here too, but Rivera has placed him on the opposite wall, for his life was long and his period of dominance came later. Here is William Silvis, the greatest of American trade union leaders, but well-nigh forgotten a generation after his death because labor does not write its own history and has not developed a continuous and cumulative tradition. Next to Silvis stands Engels, co-worker of Marx and the giver of much sound but little-heeded advice to the American labor movement of the '80's and early '90's. And overshadowing the whole panel as he overshadows the modern world stands the colossal figure of Marx.

SILVIS AND THE NATIONAL LABOR UNION

The first response of the workingmen to the new dominance of great capital after the Civil War was the foundation of the National Labor Union (1866) and its proclamation of a nation-wide drive for an eight-hour day. Its leader was William Silvis. Its formation and growth closely paralleled that of the First International. The preliminary moves for the founding of both organizations were made in 1864. Both held their first delegate meetings in 1866. Both organizations grew rapidly till the early '70's and then both disappeared, leaving behind permanent influences out of which successive movements grew.

William Silvis favored the affiliation of the National Labor Union with the First International. As president of the Union, he answered an address of the International in the following terms:

"We have a common cause. It is the war of poverty against wealth. . . . In the name of the workingmen of the United States I extend to you . . . the right hand of fellowship. Continue in the good work that you have undertaken until a glorious success shall crown your efforts! Such is our resolve. Our recent war has led to the foundation of the most infamous money aristocracy of the earth. . . . We have declared war against it and we are determined to conquer—by means of the ballot, if possible—if not, we shall resort to more serious means. A little blood-letting is necessary in desperate cases."

In 1867 the annual convention on his motion declared "its sympathy and promised its cooperation." Two years later it elected a delegate to the International.

Silvis's organization experienced a meteoric rise. Its proclamation of strikes for the eight-hour day spread with express speed from coast to coast. But the untimely death of Silvis in 1869 seriously weakened the organization. As a political movement it was absorbed by the Greenback-Populist tendency, and as a union movement it was crushed during the panic of 1873.

SHARPENING CLASS WAR

The long depression after 1873 was used by the new great-capitalist concerns to crush their weaker competitors, to smash the labor unions, to cut wages mercilessly, till at last the unorganized workers began to strike back. The struggles in the anthracite coal fields, under the leadership of a secret society, the Ancient Order of Hibernians, were smashed by the Pinkerton agency gunmen and the frame-up system. Ten of the leaders were hanged and fourteen jailed for long terms as

"Molly Maguires," that is Hibernians, on the testimony of Pinkerton agents acting as stool-pigeons, to the effect that the Hibernians aimed to murder scabs and coal barons.

The railroads were next. Here strikes spread like wildfire in 1877 against a third successive wage cut. A general strike soon tied up the Baltimore and Ohio and Pennsylvania railroads and spread to other lines. The militia was called out in seven states—the "people's militia" in a new role! In many cases the militia proved "unreliable," sympathized with and refused to fire upon the strikers, even fraternized with them. In Pittsburgh, the strikers, supported by the local militia and the entire populace, chased the imported troopers out of town; in Reading and St. Louis the same thing occurred. The fury and fright of the ruling class knew no bounds. President Hayes called out the army, the first time that the army of the United States was used to break a strike in time of peace. Unionism was outlawed. The militia was reorganized on the basis of class differentiation (the formation of the "Diamond" 7th Regiment dates from this event) and numerous strong armories were constructed in the industrial centers—fortresses for civil warfare. The new mood of workers and employers and this new phase of sharpening class struggle, Rivera has painted in the background of Panel VII (the mounted police breaking a strike), of Panel VIII (the Haymarket affair), and the entire surface of Panel IX.

THE KNIGHTS OF LABOR

As America began climbing out of the long depression of 1873, a new labor movement appeared upon the scene. All open unionism having been outlawed, the workingmen began to flock into secret fraternal orders, where signs, passwords, ritual, and oaths of secrecy were a partial protection against victimization. This was the origin of the Knights of Labor which dominated the labor scene in the 80's and whose Grand Master Workman, Terence V. Powderly, Rivera has painted between Silvis and Henry George. The Knights of Labor included both skilled and unskilled workers. It won many strikes and soon became a great power. But its pseudo-socialism (it was going to compete capitalism out of existence through cooperatives), its flirtations with middle-class populism, the timidity of its leaders who feared struggle and favored arbitration, and the savage attack of the new trusts upon all organization, especially the mass organization of the unskilled, weakened it seriously. It then engaged in a jurisdictional fight with the slowly rising organization of the skilled workers in the American Federation of Labor, and as the star of the latter rose, that of the Knights of Labor set. Powderly ended his days in a minor appointive position in the Department of Labor.

HENRY GEORGE

Henry George was hailed by his disciples as representing the rising sun of a new day. He was really a belated disciple of Paine and Jefferson and John Taylor, a representative of the dying afterglow of 18th century liberalism and physiocratic theory. An autodidact who picked up most of his education in random fashion in printing-plant and newspaper work, he proclaimed as a new discovery a doctrine of which he knew neither the long history nor its refutation. Last of a long line of land reformers, he reflected the longing for frontier democracy when the frontier was already vanishing, and proclaimed a holy war against monopoly and speculation in land, when monopoly in industry and speculation in stocks were overshadowing the whole sky. Blinded by the growing evils of capitalism, repulsed and horrified by the sharpening class struggle, he averted his gaze and anxiously concentrated his attention on an undoubtedly evil but minor excrescence of capitalism, speculation in land. Of surplus value he knew nothing. Against one of its distributive shares, ground rent, he levelled all his blows. When there was no longer enough land in America for all men, he proclaimed "the equal right of all men to use the land." As the struggle between capital and labor sharpened, he urged the community of interest of capital and labor. If only all of the share of surplus value which was going to the monopolists of land, went to the state, there would be no conflict between the producers and the monopolists of the other means of production, machinery. In the 18th century the theory of the *impôt unique* had at least been the expression of the hatred felt by the rising capitalist class for the landowners. But now the owners of capital are largely the owners of land as well, and George wanted to leave undisturbed their monopoly of the means of production and their consequent lordship over those who had to use those means of production, and yet expected all the evils of capitalism to disappear by a simple shift in the tax burden. Yet so restless was the America of his day, so heartsick at the ominous future and nostalgic for the agrarian past, that his *Progress and Poverty* became a best-seller and his campaign for mayor of New York was probably defeated only by counting him out. His service, to call attention to the strange phenomenon of the polarity of wealth and poverty, "deepening poverty amidst advancing wealth," and to carry economics out of classroom orthodoxy into the heterodoxy of the street and the public forum, and his temporary influence over the labor and populist movements, have earned him a place in Rivera's murals, as one of the many conflicting voices that sought to point a way out of the wilderness. But historically, his was the way of retreat.

HAYMARKET

Another reaction to the sharpening class war and the savage suppression of unionism was the readiness of impatient and desperate sections of the inexperienced working class to listen to the rhetorical preaching of sporadic violence, the eulogizing of dynamite as the weapon which makes labor immediately equal to capital despite the latter's monopoly of arsenals and troops, the siren song of an apocalyptic revolution which was to end capitalism overnight without any need of seizure of political power, without any need of a transition state in which the workers would rule. This amorphous doctrine of anarchism was preached in America largely to immigrants by the German refugee, Johann Most. But in altered form, with less dependence on phrase-revolutionism and more labor-organization—a kind of socialist syndicalism—it spread rapidly among certain sections of the American labor movement, above all in Chicago.

In 1884, these leaders began an agitation for the eight-hour day, as did the budding American Federation of Labor. Both the Chicago Central Labor Union and the Federation set May 1, 1886 as the date for a general strike whereafter all workers would refuse to work more than eight hours a day. The strike wave rose, and while little anarchist sheets lovingly *talked* violence, the Chicago police, the Pinkertons, and the armed forces of capital, unhesitatingly *practiced* it. Six men died under the volley of police fire on a picket line at the McCormick Harvester works.

On May 4, 1886, a protest meeting against this attack was held in the Haymarket and addressed by Spiess, Parsons, and Fielden. The Mayor and Police Chief, who were present till near the end of the meeting, pronounced the affair peaceful, and went to bed. Rain was beginning to fall and disperse the meeting when the police attacked. From somewhere a bomb was hurled. The police began firing, wounding each other as well as bystanders. Seven police were killed; how many workers, was never determined. And every outstanding labor leader in Chicago was put on trial for his life. Fielden, Parsons, Spiess, Schwab, and leaders of the Workingmen's Party, Fischer, Engel, Lingg, Neebe, Seligeri and Schnaubelt were indicted. Schnaubelt escaped. Seligeri turned "State's evidence" and was freed. No charge was made that any of the indicted had killed any one. No evidence linked them with the bomb, which has since been generally recognized as the work of a provocator. The only charge was that their speeches and writings were responsible for the tragedy. The pillars of society, bankers and manufacturers, whipped up a frenzy against them. A hand-picked jury found the defendants guilty; labor-hating Judge Gary sentenced them to death. Lingg killed himself in jail by exploding a dynamite cartridge between his teeth. Spiess, Parsons, Fischer, and Engel died on the gallows. As the noose was placed about his neck, Spiess declared: *"The time will come when our silence in the grave will be more eloquent than speeches."*

They were hanged first and investigated afterward, and then Governor John P. Altgeld proclaimed their innocence. Fielden and Schwab, whose sentences had been commuted to life imprisonment, and Neebe who got 15 years for the crime of contributing funds to a labor paper, were pardoned. Thus the Molly Maguire case and the Haymarket case initiated the long line of frame-ups which include Moyer, Haywood and Pettibone (Panel IX), the war-time prisoners (Panel XI), Tom Mooney, Sacco and Vanzetti and the Scottsboro boys (Panel XII). Rivera has painted the Haymarket martyrs with the hangman's noose about their necks, and in the upper background, Fielden speaking as the police attack begins and the bomb is thrown.

The eight-hour strikes of May Day 1886 aroused the workers throughout Europe. The Haymarket victims consecrated the struggle with their blood. Thus originated International May Day which Samuel Gompers has interdicted as "un-American"! And each year on the First of May the workers of all lands go out on strike in memory of the Chicago martyrs, in emulation of the great American labor struggle of 1886, and in token of the solidarity of the workers throughout the world.

WITH the growth of the great trusts in the closing years of the 19th century, came an enormous sharpening of the class struggle. The gigantic monopolies that were so ruthlessly crushing their competitors were certainly no tenderer with their workingmen than with rival members of their own class. Lockouts and black-lists, industrial spy systems and armed guards, injunctions and indictments, use of militia and troops, all date from this period. The whole might of the new industrial ruling class and all its resources for controlling press and opinion and governmental apparatus and private bands of armed retainers, was mobilized to crush once and for all working-class organization in the basic industries. The struggle over wages, hours, working conditions, and the right to organize, took on all the imposing grandeur of civil war.

The employers, fewer in numbers than the workers, organized earlier and more easily, built their chambers of commerce and manufacturers' and executives' associations, and assumed the offensive. The workers fought back, but they were inexperienced, badly and often treacherously led, divided by nationality, race, color, creed, and craft, unaccustomed to think and act on a national and class scale, and with little resources for undertaking nation-wide, class-wide organization.

Not only were the courts and the armed forces at the disposal of their opponents, but even the very newspapers they read, and believed, prejudiced the minds of all those not yet in struggle, against the sectors of their class already under fire. As a result, they fought on the whole a losing battle, and the basic trustified industries of America remain largely unorganized to the present day. Nevertheless, the labor movement of the '90's and early 1900's wrote some imperishable pages in the history of labor's struggles, contributed an inspiring tradition

AMERICAN
WESTERN FEDERATION OF MINERS
I.W.W.
INDUSTRIAL WORKERS OF THE WORLD
KARL MARX

that is still alive today, fashioned such organizations as have been able to survive the attack of the employers, and produced out of their ranks the first great leaders of the modern American working class.

Rivera has painted these leaders, Eugene V. Debs (center), Daniel De Leon (slightly below and to the left, with Marx's writings in his hand) and Bill Haywood (facing the bayonet to the right of Debs), and has made them the triangular keystone of his portrayal of the period. Around them are striking coal miners and metal miners, Pinkertons being disarmed (the men with raised hands) and soldiers coming to their support, striking steel workers and railroad workers. The background shows scenes from the Homestead strike and the Pullman strike, representing and telescoping together a whole series of strikes in the basic industries. And the upper background is dark with the smoke of modern industry and dark with the gathering, threatening clouds of class war.

THE HOMESTEAD STRIKE

The year of the beginning of the great offensive of organized capital against the labor movement may be set as 1892. The modern steel trust was just emerging as Carnegie Brothers and Company, and under the management of H. C. Frick, former owner of the largest coke manufacturing plant, it prepared to give battle to the Amalgamated Association of Iron and Steel Workers. The labor movement found itself face to face for the first time with a really modern corporation with practically boundless resources of war. The battle opened with a wage cut, a lockout, and the construction of a wall around the plant, three miles long, fifteen feet high, surmounted by barbed wire, and with portholes at suitable heights for the firing of guns.

Homestead was an industrial town of 12,000, almost all steel workers and their families. As the news spread that the company with which they had contractual relations and which they had enriched, was importing 300 gunmen to man this industrial fortress, to make war upon them, excitement rose high. The Pinkerton men were brought up the Monongahela River on scows at 4 A. M. on a July morning. The workingmen, warned in advance, hastily armed as best they might, barricaded the waterfront, and resisted the landing of the hostile forces. A pitched battle ensued in which at least half a dozen men on both sides were killed (some accounts give ten workers and one detective) and a number seriously wounded. The Pinkertons were disarmed and driven away. There was no further disorder, but six days later the state militia appeared. Martial law was proclaimed in Homestead, and after a four-months' siege, the strike was broken. Rivera has portrayed the battle at the river-front, the disarming of the Pinkertons, and the calling up by the Corporation of its "governmental reserves," the militia.

The same year saw the militia used to break the strike of the miners in Tennessee, the switchmen in Buffalo; President Cleveland sent in federal troops after gunmen proved ineffective and the militia "unreliable" against the striking miners of Cœur d'Alene, Idaho. The war was on!

NEW LEADERS

Organized labor now began to understand the overwhelming strength of the employing class. Out of the comprehension of the problems involved was generated the first genuine leadership that the modern American working class has developed. The aim of this new leadership was to develop class solidarity, to break down craft divisions, racial and national and local prejudices, to face the huge mergered corporations with amalgamated industrial unions equal to coping with them, to meet the chambers of commerce and manufacturers' associations with the solidarity of a united working class, and to face the employers' control of the state apparatus with some sort of political organization that could make a bid for state power.

This was not all formulated or comprehended so consciously. Different degrees of comprehension were developed by different leaders, corresponding to different viewpoints and sections of the working class. Haywood reacted to the use of the governmental power by developing a socialist-syndicalist philosophy. Debs evolved from craft unionism to industrial unionism and from populism to often-confused but always revolutionary political socialism. De Leon elaborated a rather dogmatic form of Marxist revolutionary socialism, curiously fused with syndicalism. All three stood for industrial as against craft unionism, for militancy as against compromise, for Socialism as against Capitalism. All three were dearly loved and loyally followed by many thousands of workers. All three, Debs less than the others, made the fatal mistake, after several efforts to the contrary, of giving up the task of merging or amalgamating the existing workers' organizations into more effective unions, and tried the "get-rich-quick" process of setting up brand new, rival "revolutionary unions," thereby abandoning the mass organizations to conservative and corrupt leadership. This fatal blood-letting process of dual unionism served in the long run only to drain off the progressive and radical workers from the mass unions, which explains their steady degeneration, and explains also why the views of Debs, De Leon and Haywood, so influential at first, did not leave a deeper impress on the American labor movement.

TOWARDS INDUSTRIAL UNIONISM

The victories of the employers at Homestead, Buffalo, Cœur d'Alene and the Tennessee coal mines all pointed the same lesson. Jurisdictional fights were suicidal: they benefited only the employers. The craft form was antiquated and powerless to cope with the huge corporation. New methods and new forms of organization were necessary if the labor movement were to survive in the basic industries.

The metal miners in 1893, following their defeat at Cœur d'Alene, amalgamated the several unions in their industry and formed the Western Federation of Miners. It was in this militant industrial union that Bill Haywood rose to leadership in the American labor movement.

After the defeat of the Railway Switchmen at Buffalo because the other railway unions had refused to back them up, thereby in effect backing up the employers, Eugene V. Debs, popular Grand Secretary and Treasurer and beloved, trusted leader of the Brotherhood of Railway Firemen, resigned his $4,000-a-year office against the unanimous protest of his convention, to begin the organization of an all-inclusive industrial union on the railroads, the American Railway Union. Its growth was phenomenal. Within a year it had 465 local lodges and a membership of 150,000. Not merely the employers, but the officials of the railroad brotherhoods and Samuel Gompers as well, were in a panic. Early in 1894 the union undertook a strike on the Great Northern and in eighteen days brought that powerful system to its knees.

THE PULLMAN STRIKE

The railroad companies now laid plans in secret sessions of a newly formed General Managers' Association to crush the A. R. U. When the miserably paid workers in the Pullman Palace Car Company shops at Pullman, Illinois, after receiving a cut, joined the A. R. U., they were locked out and the struggle began. The A. R. U. responded with a decision to handle no Pullman cars on any railroad till the company consented to arbitrate or treat with its employes. The strike soon tied up twenty-four lines, every railroad centering in Chicago, and drew in members of the railway brotherhoods in spite of the sabotage of the brotherhood leaders.

President Cleveland rushed troops into Illinois over the protest of Governor Altgeld. Troops and militia were used everywhere. At the height of the strike, it was estimated that there were over 14,000 soldiers, deputy marshalls, deputy sheriffs and "special agents," engaged in intimidating the strikers in the Chicago region. By decision of a secret session of the General Managers' Association, as Debs's lawyers later proved, Pinkerton agents initiated violence, burned freight cars and roundhouses, planted bombs. Several hundred arrests were made and Debs and others were indicted for various crimes, including conspiracy and murder. When the railways learned that

Clarence Darrow and Debs's other attorneys had somehow gotten the minutes of their secret session, the trial was abruptly ended on the plea that a juror had suddenly been taken sick. As far as the records show, the juror is still sick, for no effort was ever made to impanel a new jury or revive the case.

THE INJUNCTION

Now the railroads wheeled into position a new species of heavy artillery—the injunction. This remedy in "equity" for employers who could not find "adequate remedy at law" was first applied to labor disputes during this period. In 1888 a Massachusetts court enjoined the displaying of "banners with devices" in a strike. The method proved very popular and injunctions began to issue against circulars, against boycott, against informing workers that a strike was in progress, against speaking to employes, against giving food and assistance to strikers, against anything and everything needed to conduct a strike or organize a union. Judges threw off the mask and robe of "impartiality" and revealed themselves as the open representatives of the rights of property against the rights of the workers. The injunctions issue from judges who are both judge and jury, and once disobeyed, the judge, not the corporation, is the injured party. He metes out punishment, again without jury trial, not for violation of some law but for violation of his own order. The crime is a survival of *lèse majesté*—"contempt of court."

The injunction issued in the Pullman strike forbade Debs and his fellow officers to continue organizing and in effect outlawed the strike. Of course Debs and his associates violated the injunction, continued organizing and were promptly arrested for contempt of court, held six months without a hearing, then sentenced by the same judge to six months in jail.

Debs spent the six months meditating on his experiences, on the role of president and troops and courts, reading labor and Socialist pamphlets and books, studying Volume I of *Capital,* presented to him while in jail. His elementary school had been the trade unions, and in the Brotherhood of Locomotive Firemen he rose "to the head of his class." His high school had been his experience in the A. R. U., where he learned the lesson of the superiority of industrial to craft unions in fighting the modern corporation. His college was Woodstock jail where he learned the role of the state in the class struggle and the need of a workers' government. When he left Woodstock he took a brief post-graduate course of a year supporting the Bryan campaign of 1896, where he lost his last populist illusions, and then went over to Socialism where he remained as its most beloved and revolutionary figure till the day of his death. He died broken in health by another jail sentence served during the World War. He presents a living picture of how the class struggle educates the most intelligent American workers to class consciousness. Hence Rivera has made him the central figure of the panel.

BIG BILL HAYWOOD

A no less beloved leader who rose from the ranks of the American working class was William D. Haywood, popularly known as Big Bill. A hard-hitting, clear-headed western metal miner, he led many valiant battles of the Western Miners' Federation against the big silver, copper, iron, coal and lead companies of the West, where the lawless companies used huge private armies of gunmen and gangsters, regiments of detectives private and public, whole batallions of militia and stacks of injunctions, indictments, conspiracy charges and murder frame-ups.

The most celebrated of the frame-ups was the Moyer-Haywood-Pettibone case, charging Moyer, President of the Western Federation of Miners, Haywood, its secretary-treasurer, and Pettibone with the murder of the ex-governor of Idaho, Steunenberg, on the testimony of Pinkerton stool-pigeons headed by the notorious James Macparland who had begun his career by swearing away the lives of the Mollie Maguires. The case began with a brazen kidnapping of the defendants, without warrant or extradition papers, from Denver to Boise, Idaho. President Roosevelt immediately denounced them, before the trial, as "undesirable citizens." William E. Borah led the prosecution; Clarence Darrow the defense. The workers everywhere rallied to their support. The verdict was a unanimous one of "not guilty," but while Haywood was in jail, the newly-formed I. W. W. split into factions, dropped its "political action" clause, and began to crumble; the Western Federation of Miners withdrew from the I. W. W., lost in membership and morale, and Moyer, always unreliable, was frightened by his nearness to the electric chair into a conservatism which soon caused the degeneration of the Western Federation of Miners. In that sense, the frame-up was a "success," as was the jailing of Debs in the breaking of the Pullman strike. Rivera has painted Moyer, co-defendant with Haywood, to the left of Debs and De Leon.

Haywood, along with Debs, led the left wing of the Socialist Party till its growing conservatism disgusted him into withdrawing. When the Western Federation broke with the I. W. W., he elected to stay with the latter, and led it until his jailing with 92 other I. W. W. leaders at the beginning of the World War. (See Panel XI.) In jail he became a Communist, and while out on appeal, pending a new trial, and broken in health, escaped to the Soviet Union where he spent the last few years of his life. Along with John Reed, he lies buried under the Kremlin Wall in the great Red Square in Moscow. Like Debs, he is a symbol of the new type hero and working-class leader that twentieth-century America produces, and their careers epitomize and project the development of the American workers from bourgeois ideology to consciousness of the interests and role of their class.

DANIEL DE LEON

The third of Rivera's triangle of Labor leaders is a less stirring, but an important figure. A Columbia lecturer in international law who turned Socialist, he devoted his life thenceforward to the Socialist Labor Party. A powerful mind, he is one of the few Socialist leaders of the Second International who made original contribution to the theory of Marxism. His defects, a tendency to pedantic abstraction and a gift of making enemies of all whom he could not make into devoted followers, left a heavy heritage upon the movement he led. His sectarian dogmatism on the one hand and the confusion and opportunism of his opponents on the other, first split the Socialist Labor Party (the Socialist Party was an offshoot), then split the I. W. W. His powerful mind served to reinforce with theoretical supports the debilitating doctrine of dual unionism, which again and again drained off the awakened and advanced workers from the main stream of the labor movement into little doctrinaire sects. On the other hand, he kept alive the light of criticism of the opportunistic doctrines and practices which crumbled the Socialist Party with dry rot. When he died, his little sect developed no further, but lives today only as the elongated shadow of a great man. But he lives on in another sense, for his sharp, clear criticisms of the opportunism of the Socialist Party had a profound influence on the new left wing that developed in that movement during the World War, and out of which grew the Communist Party. All three of the leading heroes of this panel, Debs, Haywood, and De Leon, left their impress, defects as well as virtues, on that movement which became, in the post-war period, the heir to their heroic traditions.

PANEL X MODERN INDUSTRY

THE fashionable detestation of the machine among those who are bewildered by modern social forces, is not shared by Rivera. He is fascinated by the machine and loves to paint it "in motion." He sees in it a marvelous creation of the productive labor of mankind, a powerful and obedient servant of the producers in the mastery of nature, a thing of great esthetic beauty in its firmness and precision, in the might and subtlety of its motion, in the clarity of its lines, and the unerring expression of function in its structure. He loves the hardness and elasticity of its steel, the solidity and homogeneity of its materials. The curves and movements of its pipes and chutes and belt conveyors provide for him a dynamic geometry to guide the vision, proportion the spaces, and develop the movement of his painting in this concentrated synthesis of modern industry.

America has raised the efficiency of machinery to a very high level. Inside the modern factory there is "rationalized" technique, elimination of waste motion, avoidance of wastage of material, careful planning and division of labor. It is one of America's greatest gifts to humanity, and all over Europe (even in the Soviet Union) they talk of "Americanization," "rationalization," and "Fordism."

Rivera has painted it all here, chemical laboratories and biological laboratories, the chemistry of high temperatures (metallurgy) and of low temperatures, and the belt line of men working at the great conveyors.

Yet on the whole scene, and on every section of it, are stamped two ancient marks—the mark of Mammon and the mark of Cain. The marvelous machinery is not serving human life but the exploitation and destruction of human life.

Modern industrial America is girding itself for war, preparing to enter the struggle for world hegemony. The workers behind Ford and Edison are wearing masks. The chemical laboratory above is preparing poison gases. The biological laboratory is developing war surgery. The school is pouring the poison of chauvinism into the minds of youth. And the distant background, plowed by tractors, spanned by steel towers and high tension transmission lines, crossed by a flying plane, yields in the succeeding panel a frightful harvest of all this sowing—an endless field of crosses.

From the board of directors' meeting in the upper center, and from every department of the symbolic factory and laboratories, run pipes to a hopper in the foreground. The pipes drain from all the scientific and productive activities of man, from all their sweat and toil, a constant stream of gold. The hand regulating the lever attached to the coin-hopper is the palsied hand of old John D. Rockefeller, reaching over from the next panel, as the hand of Morgan reaches over into a succeeding panel at the corresponding point on the opposite wall. Rockefeller and Morgan are figures too imposing to fit into the limits of a single panel. They are the grotesque incarnations of America's fantastic accumulation of polar wealth and poverty.

ANDREW MELLON

Next to the hand of Rockefeller appears the face of Andrew W. Mellon, ear anxiously at a telephone receiver to learn of the rise and fall of stock market values. He has earned a place here although he has not lifted a finger to produce, or even to organize the production of the great industry of America. Unlike Ford, who is identified with autos, Rockefeller with oil, the du Ponts with chemicals, he draws tribute indifferently from many industries and brought none of them into existence. Real estate, banking, railroads, and railway equipment, aluminum, electric power, oil, coal and its by-products, steel and whiskey, each pours its stream of yellow metal into the billion-dollar hoard of his family. They control or have large interests in corpora-

AFL

tions with assets of over ten billions—twice as much as all the gold there is in the United States—almost as much as the value of all the gold in the entire world. His services to himself and his class in shifting the tax burden of the great war costs from the millionaires to the mass of the people, earned him the title of "the greatest secretary of the treasury since Alexander Hamilton." The only Secretary "who ever had three presidents serve under him," he is the 20th century embodiment of Hamilton's dream—the direct rule of plutocracy.

EDISON AND FORD

No representation of modern industry would be complete without Edison and Ford. Rivera has given them the central position—the last representatives of the old-style "captain of industry" in an age when the dominant type is the master of finance and speculation, "the money king." Rivera has treated them with less severity, as men of real talent who would have been useful and important under any social system, unlike the Mellons and Morgans whose talents are merely acquisitive and predatory. They are comparable in a certain measure to the machinery and laboratories in the picture. Under a society where production existed for the sake of the producers, and not vice versa, their organizing and inventive talents, like the belt conveyor and efficiency systems, like the laboratories and machines, would serve to lighten labor, produce leisure and plenty, and set man free from the animal struggle against hunger, for the development of his specifically human capacities. But as work has been perverted from a necessity and expression of vital activity into a mere means of keeping alive, and machinery from a powerful and willing servant into a powerful and willful master, so the inventive and organizing talents of these men have been perverted into talent for monopolizing patents, organizing exploitation and speed-up, consolidating industrial serfdom, and producing the monstrous contradiction of marvelous planning within the factory for the planless pouring of a stream of goods into a planless society!

Samuel Gompers has been selected by Rivera as the "labor leader" to go with this representation of the perversion of science and technique from productive to acquisitive ends and the prostitution of culture and the "arts of peace" to the purpose of mass slaughter and imperialist war. For Samuel Gompers represents the perversion of the labor movement from the aims of labor defense and emancipation to those of class collaboration.

Vague in views, ungrounded in theory, grotesquely limited in mental horizon, Gompers nevertheless entered the labor movement as a radical. His autobiography gives reluctant testimony to the "revolutionaries in thought and deed" from whom he "learned the fundamentals of the labor movement" and to the *Communist Manifesto* that "brought me an interpretation of much that had been only inarticulate feeling." In the first conventions of the American Federation of Labor, Gompers led the radical faction and as its leader reached the post of President, which he held for over forty years. But his knowledge of revolutionary theory, gleaned from casual lectures, newspaper articles, and conversations, was not reinforced by any systematic thought or study. Within a few years he manifested a growing hardening of the intellectual arteries. His fight with the Knights of Labor developed an antagonism to the union of skilled and unskilled and to industrial unionism, which he tried to justify on "theoretical" and demagogic grounds. In 1890 he began a fight with the Socialists by refusing a charter to the New York Central Labor Union because it accepted affiliation with the Socialist Labor Party. De Leon's disastrous response was to form a rival dual union organization, draining the socialists and radicals from the A. F. of L. and enormously increasing its conservatism. In 1896 Gompers still spoke of the ultimate aim of the labor movement as the abolition of capitalism. For the last time he declared his support for the immediate struggles of the workers "even if but to gain a milestone on the thorny road to emancipation."

By 1903 he was openly denouncing the revolutionary movement: "There are employers who . . . refuse to confer . . . when they are led to believe that property is in danger of confiscation."

In 1901 he joined and became vice-president of the newly-formed National Civic Federation, organized by the notorious Mark Hanna and including such "friends" of labor as Morgan, Guggenheim, Dodge, du Pont, Ryan, Willard, Belmont.

The final step in his progress of betrayal was the harnessing of the labor movement to the war machine. In 1916, while he was still making pacifist speeches, the Army Appropriation Bill of August 29 created a Council of National Defense, including the Secretaries of War, Navy, Interior, Agriculture and Labor, and seven prominent civilians, among them Daniel Willard, Bernard M. Baruch and Samuel Gompers. Gompers, in turn, created a war committee on labor, "appointing" such men as John D. Rockefeller, Jr., to membership. And on March 12, 1917, he and his associates pronounced the coming war "labor's war" and declared:

"We, the officers of the national and international trade unions of America . . . hereby pledge ourselves in peace or in war . . . to stand unreservedly by the . . . safety and preservation of the institutions and ideals of our Republic." He had traveled far from the "thorny road of emancipation" and the days when he found inspiration and understanding in the *Communist Manifesto.*

Rivera has portrayed him as the misleader of the long line of victims of the industrial machine, in his right hand the symbols of his demagogy and in his left the petty rewards of his corruption and perversion of the labor movement to the purposes of exploitation and war.

LAND OF CONTRASTS

Rivera's portrait shows America as a land of strange contradictions: a nation proud of its achievements in science, yet wedded to the most fantastic religious superstitions; boasting of great contributions to the penetration of the secrets of nature and mastery of her processes, and full of church-going believers in miracles; magnificent libraries for the dispelling of darkness, and churches for maintaining it; universities with superb laboratories, and schools for teaching of the "science" of theology; a nation abounding in laws and famed for its lawlessness; founded on the principles of toleration and the equality of all men, and maintaining Jim-Crow laws, racial discrimination, the fiery cross, the Ku Klux Klan and lynching; land of abounding wealth, and incredible poverty; so careful of materials and instruments, so careless of human life; turning out a constant stream of goods and a constant stream of human wreckage.

All this Rivera has traced in broad strokes in the left section of this crowded portrait of modern industrial America. That is the meaning of the stream of broken men and women pouring out of the left-hand side of the factory as the stream of gold pours out of the right. That is the meaning of the inset where Millikan, great physicist and fantastic religious apologist and inventor of poison gases, is shown with the well-fed and rubicund Bishop Manning proclaiming God's enmity to the Soviet Union, and Aimee Semple Macpherson giving religion a touch of sex appeal and vaudevillianism. And that is the meaning of the background of lynching party and fiery cross and Ku Klux Klan, and the further background of bank and court house and church and armory. They are the concomitants of modern industry in present day America. Capitalism maintains them and they maintain capitalism. And out of the lordship of capital over machinery and productive labor and the state power, out of modern capitalist industry, flow all the consequences—world war, imperialism, unemployment—that Rivera has painted in the succeeding panels.

WHEN the war broke out in Europe, it took the average American by surprise. He knew nothing of the relations between imperialism and war, nor did he dream that his own country had any connection with imperialism. He congratulated himself that the United States was a republic and not a monarchy and no kaiser or king could force us into war. President Wilson proclaimed the nation "too proud to fight" and called for neutrality "in thought and deed"; the National Security League, organized in 1914 and numbering among its supporters the du Pont powder interests, the United States Steel Corporation, Vanderbilt, Guggenheim, Morgan and Rockefeller, began its preparedness drive; the J. P. Morgan Company, bankers and purchasing agents for the Allies, began floating loans with American banks at the rate of over a billion a year to finance purchases of war supplies at the rate of over $10,000,000 a day.

Inside a year the real rulers of America had tied up the American banking system and American industries so completely with the success of the Allies that the entrance of the United States into the war was a foregone conclusion, unless the Allies could win unaided.

WOODROW WILSON

Pacifist and professional idealist, professorial liberal and master phrasemonger, Woodrow Wilson was admirably suited to bringing a reluctant nation into the war. As early as January, 1915, he sent his mysterious personal emissary, Colonel House, to Europe, without consultation of Congress, much less of the people, to try to affect an early peace on terms favorable to the Allies; and by the time House returned in the summer of that year, he had already let the Allies know that if they were in danger of defeat by Germany, America would enter the war. On the 30th of May, 1915, he wrote in his diary: "I have concluded that war with Germany is inevitable." And in a conference with Briand and Jules Cambon: "I again told them that the lower the fortunes of the Allies ebbed, the closer the United States would stand by them." By the end of the year, a scheme for American entrance had been fully worked out, and a memorandum, initialed by Lord Grey and approved by Wilson with only the addition of the word "probably" before "enter the war" as a face-saver in case Congress should get possession of the memorandum, bears the date of February 22, 1916. Yet in the Fall of 1916, President Wilson ran for reelection with the slogan Rivera has pictured in the bill of the dove of peace that stands on his shoulder: "He kept us out of war."

In the foreground Rivera has given vivid portraits of the money kings who engineered the entrance into the war of the nation that had congratulated itself that it had no kings to force it into senseless slaughter. On the left, the mummy-face of John D. Rockefeller, ticker-tape in hand, and his Sunday-school-teaching son, with Clemenceau, like a pleading mastiff, begging for funds. Behind Clemenceau, the ubiquitous Colonel House, and behind him Albert, King of the Belgians and pawn on the chessboard of Allied diplomacy. In the center, Czar Nicholas with the face of an imbecile and degenerate, in his hands money stained with blood. On the right, matching Clemenceau, Lloyd George receiving the proceeds of the Morgan loans, and the Mikado, appropriate ally in the "war for democracy!" Then du Pont, the munitions maker, Bernard M. Baruch, and the master of them all, J. P. Morgan. Above them, Orlando of Italy, Venizelos of Greece, and the mysterious figure of that man without a country who sells munitions to all countries, Sir Basil Zaharoff. Behind Zaharoff stands King Peter of Serbia.

Behind America's war makers and the spokesmen of her Allies, Rivera has portrayed the symbol of the war's richest harvest. The millions of the men who made the war were converted into billions,

IN GOD WE TRUST
He Kept us out of War
RESERVE
CCCP
DOWN WITH COMPA NY UNIONISM!! SMASH ROCKEFELLER SERFDOM!

and 6,000 new millionaires were created. It was a big war, a record breaker. Over 50,000,000 young men in the prime of life—"the cream of the crop"—were put upon the battlefields, with the greatest achievements of modern science at their command, to destroy each other. Of the fifty million, ten million, one in every five, remained on the field of battle. Over 20,000,000 suffered serious wounds. To this must be added pestilence and famine and the horrible toll of human wreckage behind the lines.

The financial costs are no less impressive. The United States Treasury reckons the gross cost to this country as $51,400,000,000. The total cost to all participants has been estimated at $337 billion—surely not an overestimation. Rivera has painted the harvest of war in the famine victims with their blown-up bellies and wasted frames; in the triumphant products of plastic surgery with their grotesque fragments of faces, condemned to remain for the rest of their lives in detention camps lest the people see the nameless horror and turn in fury on the war makers; in the field of crosses row on row that forms the upper left background of the panel; in the calculating, complacent faces of Morgan and the Rockefellers and Baruch, of du Pont and Zaharoff, who harvested fresh billions from the unparalleled magnitude of financial operations and munitions orders during the war.

THE CLASS STRUGGLE IN WARTIME

The ruling class of every country demanded of its agents in the labor movement class peace, for the duration of the war.

"This is a war against war, that is what this war is. It is a crusade, a war of the enraged civilian populations defending their menaced liberties and democracies. It is not a capitalist war . . ." was the answer of Samuel Gompers. The A. F. of L. leadership signed a pact with the government that there would be no strikes for the duration of the conflict. The workers thought otherwise, but wherever they struck to make wages keep pace with sky-rocketing living costs, they

OLORADO FUEL AND IRON Co
DOWN WITH COMPA
NY UNIONISM !!
SMASH ROCKEFELLER
SERFDOM!
ONLY WORKING CLASS
VICTORY WILL CHECK
THE FLOW OF BLOOD.
WILL STOP THE
FLOOD OF TEARS.
—WILLIAM D. HAYWOOD

were crushed by the united efforts of employers, government, and labor leaders.

The consistent opponents of this class peace in the service of imperialism, were to be found only in the left wing of the Socialist Party and the I. W. W. The Government answered the strikes of the I. W. W. with a frenzied attack. Federal troops were called out against the strikers. Mobs of business men organized in "Citizens' Alliance" or "Patriotic League" kidnapped their leaders. Frank Little, a member of the General Executive Board active in the copper strike in Montana, was kidnapped from his room at night, tortured, and then hanged from a railroad trestle. Rivera shows the lynching in the upper left of the picture, against a background of marching men and flying flags. More than a thousand members of the I. W. W. were thrown into jail. In one case alone, Judge Kenesaw Mountain Landis, today "baseball czar," meted out sentences totalling 2,089 years and fines amounting to $2,660,000 to 93 leaders of the I. W. W. in a mass trial which did not even preserve the formalities of the rights of individual defense.

The left Socialists were jailed wholesale under the "Espionage Act," supposed to be aimed at German spies but so broad as to cover all activities and utterances which, in the opinion of the Government, might hinder the prosecution of the war. Rivera has portrayed Wilson, uttering his fine phrases about Democracy and bringing down his fist upon a rostrum which is at the same time a jail, through the bars of which are visible the faces of Bill Haywood, Eugene V. Debs, and Charles E. Ruthenberg.

THE RUSSIAN REVOLUTION

The war makers calculated many things in the harvest they were to reap from the war, but one thing they did not calculate. The Kaiser dreamed of "a place in the sun," of Bagdad and the Dardanelles, of Northern Africa and the distant Orient—but he did not foresee exile in Doorn! The Czar dreamed of Constantinople and the Balkans, of Persia and Northern China—but he did not dream of February and November 1917! The financiers foresaw dividends and fresh investment markets, tribute from new spheres of influence and conquered provinces, but they did not foresee the beginning of the end of the system they represent! In victorious and vanquished countries alike, the masses paid the cost of the war, paid in hunger and disease, paid in taxes and toil, supplied the toll of the wounded and the dead. But they, too, reaped some redemption from their frightful calvary, the rising star of hope in the East, a break in the system that breeds war and unemployment, one-sixth of the surface of the earth, a country where the workers rule and are laying the foundations of a new social order. The upper right hand corner of the panel is aglow with the red streamer of the Third (Communist) International, a weapon forged in the fire of war and revolution to replace the discredited Second (Socialist) International that had broken down at the beginning of the war. The red streamer flows into the red banner of the Soviet Union under whose folds are visible the marching masses of Russia's armed workers. Trotsky is reviewing the Red Army and behind him stands Lenin, the greatest leader of the Russian Revolution and of the Communist International. Beneath the streamer, in the distant background are visible the "holy" towers of the Kremlin.

FROM IMPERIALIST WAR TO CIVIL WAR

The Russian Revolution of November 1917 put an end to the war. The example of the Russian workers was contagious. The slowly growing unrest in the trenches and behind the lines of all the great powers suddenly took on enormous proportions. For a while, the German war machine continued to roll over apparently prostrate Russia on its old momentum as if nothing had happened. And then General Von Hoffmann found that his troops were being "infected." Germany negotiated a victor's peace, to release troops to the Western Front, and the "infection" spread to the West. It was spreading in the Allied armies too, but here it was somewhat slowed up by the injection of fresh blood, the arrival of the American Expeditionary Force. Yet Pershing sent many anxious dispatches to Wilson about the need of hastening the arrival of American soldiers because of mutiny among the French troops.

Our school children are taught the official myth that the war was ended by the brave American doughboys at Argonne Forest and Château Thierry. But the Hindenburg Line was not broken—it collapsed. It was not pierced from without, it crumpled from within. The war was ended by revolution.

INTERVENTION

The spread of revolution created a panic spirit in the ruling circles of victor and vanquished nations alike. The German army of occupation was instructed to remain in the Ukraine till Allied troops could relieve them. Thus did victor and vanquished unite before the menace of the "common enemy." Without the formality of a declaration of war, England, France, Japan, and the United States rushed army divisions into the country of their ally of yesterday, to aid in the overthrow of this government of workers and peasants. Rivera has painted Kerensky and Kolchak under the sheltering cloak of Woodrow Wilson as symbol of the vast quantities of money and munitions that went to them and every other counter-revolutionary adventurer that requested American aid. And above, just beneath the figures of Lenin and Trotsky and the heads of the marching bands of the Red Army, he has painted a memorable scene from American history on which the text books and the newspapers are strangely silent—a scene which Rivera had to paint from the oral description of participants—the mutiny of the Detroit troops at Archangel!

Long after other countries had ceased fighting, Russia was forced to continue. On twenty fronts the exhausted Russian masses were compelled to fight against counter-revolution supported by foreign intervention. Against them were arrayed the superior equipment and funds of the Allied war machine. Allied troops occupied Archangel and Vladivostok and the Ukraine. A French fleet steamed into the Black Sea. An iron ring, the *cordon sanitaire,* cut off a backward and ruined nation from war materials, metals, even medical supplies, disinfectants

and bandages. But the ragged, barefoot, ill-equipped armies of the Soviet Union possessed something the invading forces lacked—*morale.* They "demoralized" the forces of their opponents, opposing machine guns, tanks and gas bombs with their own invincible weapon—propaganda. The armies sent against them resolved themselves into their constituent elements—workers and peasants. The French fleet mutinied. The French troops mutinied. The British troops mutinied. The Detroit regiment that had been enlisted to "lick the Kaiser," fretting and fuming in the frozen wastes of an Archangel winter, quarreled with their British officers, wondered why they were invading an Allied country, why they couldn't go home now that the Kaiser was gone and the war was over. The Russians were glad to explain.

Then Spring came, the harbor became ice-free, but instead of being taken home the American troops were ordered to advance farther into the Russian land. The mutiny was well-nigh unplanned. The commanding officer gave the order to advance—farther away from home—and no one stirred. The officer had a machine gun wheeled into position, pointing at his troops, and told them: "When I give the command again, any man who doesn't move gets the business end of this." He gave the command, and spontaneously, as one man, every soldier raised his gun and leveled it at the commanding officer. He burst into tears, and ended by pledging his word that they would be taken home. They were, and no other troops were sent to replace them. Nor were the details of the mutiny made public or punishment attempted.

Thus ended the activities of the American Expeditionary Force. For Rivera its noblest achievement was not the victory at Château Thierry but the mutiny at Archangel.

THE era of Wilsonian rule was ushered in by a series of promises collectively known as "The New Freedom." The fulfillment of these promises Rivera has portrayed in this panel.

Gone are the trust-busting days when every politician who aspired to popularity found it necessary to take pot-shots at the "malefactors of great wealth." The war changed them into "benefactors." As dollar-a-year men they patriotically took over the government. Big business wrapped itself in the American flag, and no respectable person would fling mud at the Stars and Stripes; the "muck-raking" days were over. The new slogan was more consonant with the profit system: no longer, "Bust the trusts," but "100% Americanism."

RED RAIDS

Big business was not slow to follow up its advantage. To keep the war machinery moving smoothly, it had found itself obliged to raise wages (even though not so fast as the cost of living) and to deal with the conservative trade unions. No sooner was the war over than the enormously strengthened ruling class opened an attack, unparalleled in severity, upon all forms of labor organization.

The offensive was strategically planned. The first blow was aimed at the militant but inexperienced vanguard, the newly formed Communist movement. On November 7, 1919, while the Communists and their supporters were engaged in the "criminal" activities of dancing and applauding speeches in celebration of the second anniversary of the Russian Revolution, Attorney-General Palmer and his agents, aided by Burns men and local "bomb squads," heroically attacked every workingman's dance hall, loaded the celebrants in vans and police-wagons without troubling about the formalities of a warrant, and took them to police headquarters by the thousands. The Communist movement was driven underground and largely isolated from the labor movement into which it was just beginning to sink roots and to which it might have given militant leadership. Two of the victims of the "red hysteria" of 1919-20 were Niccolo Sacco and Bartolomeo Vanzetti.

THE OPEN SHOP DRIVE

The next step in the employing-class offensive was the open-shop drive. It was carefully prepared. It was thoroughly organized. The drive was initiated by the United States Chamber of Commerce.

"540 organizations in 247 cities of 44 states," wrote the National Founders' Association, "are engaged in promoting this American principle in employment relations. A total of 23 national industrial associations are included . . . 1,665 local chambers of commerce are also pledged to the principle of the open-shop."

In the series of defensive strikes which followed, the whole apparatus of national and state governments was mobilized by the employers. The courts issued injunctions, some of them so sweeping as to prohibit workers from calling the scabs "strikebreakers," and even to forbid workers to sit on their own porches when the strikebreakers were passing by on their way to or from work.

The Attorney General of the United States Harry M. Daugherty proclaimed: *"So long and to the extent that I can speak for the government of the United States, I will use the power of the government within my control to prevent the labor unions of the country from destroying the open shop. . . ."*

President Harding called out the troops, openly incited the railways and mines to employ strikebreakers and the governors to use the state militias, and assumed the role of commander-in-chief of America's business men in the big offensive for the breaking of labor's line of defense and the winning of the open shop, rebaptized "American Plan." Such was the industrial serfdom that jailed America's militants,

tied labor's hands, and fettered them to the machine. Such was the fulfillment of the promises of the "New Freedom" in the "world fit for heroes to live in."

LABOR IN CHAINS

This picture reflects and enlarges the signs of enslavement and oppression in the corresponding panel (panel V) on the opposing wall. There Thoreau was in jail, here Tom Mooney looks through the grating of his cell. There a Negro was being whipped, another shot, and a third in stocks; here the nine Scottsboro boys are in prison, a worker in shackles is being lashed, Sacco and Vanzetti are seated in the electric chair, and the Statue of Liberty itself is seen through the prison bars. There slaves are seen in chains and iron collars; here "free" workers are handcuffed to the machines at which they labor. The handcuffs are no mere painter's symbolism, but a faithful copy of a highly efficient modern punch press which is worked by manacled workers whose hands are automatically pulled back by the handcuffs every time the punch press descends. This prevents mashing of the hands by the press, a costly interruption of the work, and at the same time automatically regulates the speed of the hands so that no matter how tired the worker may become, the handcuffs guarantee the same invariant rhythm—in the case of this particular machine, over 1,000 punches an hour. The advertising literature which provided Rivera's "model" boasted that the machine would yield "12,000 punches in a 9-hour day—as many punches per hour in the last hour as in the first."

TOM MOONEY

Tom Mooney was really the first victim of the war hysteria, but his prolonged imprisonment and heroic attitude have made him the dramatic symbol of the post-war "New Freedom." On July 22, 1916, during the series of preparedness parades that were meant to engineer America's entrance into the war, some provocator or madman threw a bomb at the parade in San Francisco. The district attorney's office made no attempt to find the real culprit, but seized Thomas Mooney, Mrs. Rena Mooney, Warren K. Billings, and Israel Weinberg, charging them with murder. The Pacific Gas and Electric Company, the power company that controls California, had made several efforts to "frame" Mooney before, because of his leadership in the Molders' Union, in the car strike, and the fight of San Francisco labor against the open-shop drive. Their special agents moved into the district attorney's office and prepared the case. Witnesses were manufactured, perjured testimony was secured from men who were themselves in fear of police prosecution for crime and who thus purchased immunity, and Mooney was condemned "to be hanged by the neck until dead."

Then the case began to crumble. Suppressed pictures revealed Mooney to have been over a mile away watching the parade at the very moment the explosion occurred. The government witnesses admitted perjury and told how they had been coached and bribed by the prosecution. The jurors repented their verdict and the ten still living have since pleaded for a pardon for the condemned man. The judge who presided at the trial expressed his shame that his court had been used for such purposes. Two presidential commissions, one under Wilson, one under Hoover, declared Mooney innocent. But he is still in jail.

Were it not for the huge protest strikes in the United States and the great demonstrations throughout the world, he would long be in his grave. The Russian demonstrations especially, occurring after the first Russian Revolution of February, 1917, when Russia's further participation in the war was hanging in the balance and Wilson was trying to persuade the Russian masses that the war was a war for democracy, caused the President's intervention to prevent the hanging of Mooney. The governor of California graciously commuted the sentence of the innocent man to life imprisonment!

Mooney was arrested in 1916. The California industrialists, aided by corrupt labor leaders and cynical politicians in judge's robes and governor's chairs, have kept him in jail while his wife grows old and gray waiting for him outside, and while Tom Mooney watches the years of his vigorous young life slowly slipping away from him in his living tomb. Eighteen years this innocent man has lost so far—a living monument to capitalist justice, to the arrogance of big business, to the impotence of a divided, disorganized, misled labor movement to defend and liberate one of its own. He has been offered a parole, but a parole is an admission of guilt and carries with it a prohibition from participation in the labor movement. They would free his body and chain his soul. "I will rot and die within the walls of San Quentin Prison before I will accept a degrading and humiliating parole that would make me a conditional prisoner for life," he writes. From his jail he fights on, sending out letter after letter, pamphlet after pamphlet, appealing for the unity of the labor movement, for purification from corrupt leadership, for the labor loyalty and courage of which his own conduct in his living tomb has been a splendid example.

THE SCOTTSBORO CASE

Rivera has painted the Scottsboro boys as a symbol of how the post-war world has been made "fit for heroes to live in," if the heroes' skins are black. Nine Negro boys were arrested and eight of them convicted and sentenced to death for the alleged "raping" of two white prostitutes, one of whom has since confessed that she was lying. They were convicted on evidence for which the word "flimsy" would be a gross exaggeration. There have been the usual frame-up methods, and the frame-up structure has not been able to hold together. Yet the prosecutor asked for and got a conviction on their second trial because they were "guilty as hell" of being black, and their lawyer "a Jew from New York." Their "case" has been shuttling back and forth between the higher and lower courts since March, 1931, but they are still in jail and will die there, unless an aroused and united protest sets them free.

Since 1882, the first year in which any attempt was made to gather statistics on lynching, over 4,000 Negroes, including 75 women, have been either hanged or burned, or hanged and then burned, by "lynch" law. But the number of those who have been "legally" lynched, after a farcical trial like that of the Scottsboro boys, is even greater. These Negro boys have become the dramatic symbol of the fight against "legal" and "illegal" lynching alike, the fight against all forms of racial discrimination and oppression, the fight for full economic, political, and social equality for black and white, without which there can be no real freedom in America.

THE SACCO-VANZETTI CASE

If the Mooney case represents the first tender shoot of the new freedom the war for democracy was to bring to America, the Sacco-Vanzetti case represents the full fruition.

In the "red raids" of 1919-20, these two Italian labor organizers of philosophical anarchist affiliation were arrested and charged with payroll robbery and murder! As in the Mooney case, there was no attempt to apprehend the real criminals. The seizure of the strike leader Vanzetti was far more important. So too was the conviction of the shoe-worker-organizer Sacco more important than that of a mere payroll robber. The farcical substitute for a trial accorded these two men has been analyzed by the distinguished jurist, Felix Frankfurter: "certainly in modern times Judge Thayer's opinion stands unmatched for discrepancies between what the record discloses and what the opinion conveys." Tried for robbery and murder, and convicted of radical labor activities! Yet the whole machinery of "justice" was mobilized to see that these two men were electrocuted. The Supreme Court refused to intervene, the liberal Judge Brandeis included. Governor Fuller, President Lowell of Harvard (pictured by Rivera as giving the academic blessing), President Stratton of Massachusetts Institute of Technology, Judge Robert Grant, "confirmed" the farcical verdict and the criminal sentence. As the tide of protest rose, Judge Thayer said: "Those bastards down there trying to intimidate me. . . . I'll get them good and proper. . . . I'd like to hang a few dozen of the radicals."

The protest on behalf of the condemned was hampered by divisions in the labor movement. The local defense committee tried till too near the end to prevent mass demonstrations and to leave the accused to the tender mercies of the courts. The protest rose in a mighty wave throughout the world, but it rose too late. On August 23, 1927, after seven years, four months and fourteen days of legal torture, with all the luxurious paraphernalia of modern science, these two gentle heroes suffered death by the passage of a current of electricity through their bodies. To Judge Thayer, Vanzetti declared: *"If it had not been for this thing, I might have lived out my life, talking at street corners to scorning men. I might have died, unmarked, unknown, a failure. Now we are not a failure. This is our career and our triumph. . . . Our words—our lives—our pains—nothing! The taking of our lives—lives of a good shoemaker and a poor fish peddler—all! That last moment belongs to us—that agony is our triumph."*

The open-shop drive, industrial serfdom, frame-up and third degree, Mooney, the Scottsboro boys, Sacco and Vanzetti—such is the image Rivera has painted of the "New Freedom" that has come to America as the result of its crusade to make the rest of the world "safe for democracy."

A LONG line of battleships leads from the remote background of the picture to the flag ship whose huge cannon seem to jut out from the painted wall. They overshadow the idyllic islands of the Caribbean where two bloody hands have left their stain. They form a central triangle with the staff of the Star-Spangled Banner and the up-thrust nozzle of the gun of an armored tank. They form two sides of another triangle filled by the American eagle clutching the earth in its talons, its breast-plate a dollar sign, and beneath its outspread wings the legend—"N. Y. Stock Exchange." The two hemispheres and the dollar sign form a familiar combination—three balls, the sign of the pawnbroker—"Uncle Shylock" the world calls him—who lends huge sums at appropriate interest against the pledge of the sovereignties, the resources, and the liberties of nations, and collects arrears and forfeited pledges with the aid of the United States marines.

Just behind the American flag may be seen the warehouse of the United Fruit Company, master of the banana empire of Central America, and the oil derricks of the Standard Oil Company, whose far-flung pipe-line empire reaches into Mexico and Venezuela and Peru and Colombia and the desperately disputed oil-bearing jungle swamp of El Gran Chaco, and beyond Latin America into Europe, Asia, and Africa. From the patient sad-eyed burro at the right of the warehouse of the United Fruit Company, there flows a deep golden river of bananas on the crest of which float baskets of pineapples and other tropical fruits. Beyond are the banana trees and the fields of sugar cane where peons wield the sharp *machete*. The tropical luxuriance is adorned with the bodies of rebel peons hanging from telegraph poles.

The upper background shows American marines "restoring order"

STANDARD
OIL Co
OF NEW YORK
UNITED FRUIT Co
WEST INDIES
STOCK
EX
CHANGE

or "guaranteeing orderly processes of government," somewhere or other in Latin America, so cursed by its rich blessings of oil and gold and tropical vegetation, and fateful nearness to the Panama Canal.

After America embarked on world empire with the Spanish-American war and the seizure of Cuba, Porto Rico, and the Philippines, more than thirty times did American marines land in the countries of Central America in the first quarter of the 20th century, making and unmaking governments, forcing reluctant borrowings and collecting on loans, supervising elections and outlawing nationalist patriot candidates, seizing customs houses and installing military administrators and financial advisers, establishing protectorates and writing treaties with bayonets. The battleships belching smoke and fire, the bombing planes teaching respect and submission to obstinate lovers of liberty, the machine guns and villages in flames in the background, and the advancing line of tanks, and marines firing from behind sandbags in the foreground, are a composite picture of the thirty-odd, too importunate gifts of the blessings of Yankee freedom and investment and supervision to Mexico, Central America and the Caribbean.

TROPICAL RHYTHMS

The opulent rhythms of the luxuriant tropical fruits of the background are echoed in the rhythms of sand bags and dead bodies of Hispano-American patriots in the foreground, while out of the carnage there is distinguishable the face of a dead Central American Negro, any one of the 3,250 Haitians killed by the marines during the five years of American occupation between 1915 and 1920, or of the Dominicans, Cubans, or other Caribbean peoples. Next to him is the dead face of the brilliant young Cuban Communist and student-leader, Julio Antonio Mella, who was assassinated in Mexico by the gunmen of the butcher Machado, maintained in Cuba so many years by the support of American capital and the State Department.

SANDINO

Over the whole panel broods the grim and determined face of the patriot hero ("bandit," Secretary of State Stimson called him) Augusto Cesar Sandino. Every age, every struggle, produces its heroes—what Wallace and Bruce were for Scotland, what Emmet and Wolfe Tone and Connolly were for Ireland, what Mazzini and Garibaldi were for Italy, what Gabriel and Denmark Vesey and Nat Turner were for the enslaved Negroes of America and Toussaint L'Ouverture for the Negroes of Haiti, that Sandino was, not merely for Nicaragua, but for the whole of Latin America.

DAVID AND GOLIATH

Latin America had long been smoldering with hostility at the aggression of the mighty "Colossus of the North." But how could the nations of Spanish America resist the "almighty dollar" backed by the imposing array of force of the greatest army and navy in the New World? America rode roughshod over country after country, for the Yankee power was irresistible.

But then a "miracle" occurred, like the "miracle" of David and Goliath. Little Nicaragua, whose offense against the United States had been the possession of an alternative route to the Panama Canal, little Nicaragua that had had three governments overthrown by American marines, that had had loans forced upon it, and constitutions set aside by the American State Department because they prohibited foreign loans, that had been forced at the cannon's mouth to accept the "protection" of the United States, that had been made to yield Fonseca Bay as a naval base and the concession of a trans-isthmian canal, that had been overrun by American marines from 1912 to 1925 and had been invaded again in 1926—little Nicaragua with an area of 49,000 square miles and a population under a million—Nicaragua decided to resist!

For more than five years, Augusto Sandino and his heroic bands held out against the American marines in his mountain fastness of

El Chipote. Aeroplanes, gas bombs, all the splendor of modern warfare were used against him. His mountains, the sympathy and the support of his entire people, the courage and the morale that comes to those who fight for freedom, fought on his side. It cost the United States Marine Corps more than 130 lives and millions of dollars above its usual budget, but they could not defeat Sandino.

The spell was broken. The brazen giant of the North was revealed to have feet of clay. If American imperialism had seemed irresistible,

it was but the disunity of the Latin American peoples, the cowardice, the corruption, the treachery of their governments and ruling classes, their unwillingness to arm the masses of workers and peasants for guerrilla warfare which made it so.

The prostrate Latin American lands began to grow restless, stirred by the inspiration of Sandino's audacious war. The situation became untenable for the army of occupation. Either the nation of 120,000,000 would have to declare war upon the nation of 600,000 and mobilize its army and navy in earnest, or the marines would have to withdraw.

In 1932, the marines withdrew, leaving Sandino unbeaten, in possession of the field. As naïve politically as he was courageous, the hero of El Chipote disarmed all but 100 of his followers, abandoned his mountain fortress, and embarked on a cooperative farming project with his comrades. The marines had withdrawn, but they left behind them a national guard trained by American officers, and Sacasa, an American tool, as president of Nicaragua. Sandino moved around the country without guile or suspicion. He even accepted an invitation to dine with the President to discuss the affairs of the nation. On leaving the presidential palace, he was seized by the national guard and shot by a firing squad. Treachery had accomplished what the marines could not. And appropriately enough, Washington's birthday was chosen by the agents of American imperialism to assassinate this "father of his country" and of Latin American freedom.

When the epoch of imperialism is over, when the Latin American masses have learned to combine against foreign aggression and native treachery, and have cemented their alliance with the opponents of imperialism north of the Rio Grande, the workers and poor farmers of the United States, then Sandino will be remembered as the great precursor, the first of the battlers for a free American continent. Therefore Rivera has painted him in this panel, not merely as the hero of a Nicaraguan episode, but as the symbol of the struggle against American imperialism.

PANEL XIV DEPRESSION

HUNGER and want man has often known in the past. Fat years have been followed by lean years and men have starved and suffered. But that was hunger due to scarcity, due to pestilence, drought or flood. Men and women knew why they were hungry then—they went hungry because of a failure of the imperfect productive forces of man and the uncontrollable forces of nature.

Only under industrial capitalism, which has marvelously augmented his productive powers, has man learned to know this fantastic phenomenon that Rivera has tried to convey to us here—the contradictory, incredible apparition of starvation in the midst of surfeit, of hunger because there is too much! The forces of production have outgrown the limitations imposed upon them by the structure of capitalism, and every time they begin to expand, they meet absolute barriers which they cannot break through so long as capitalism endures.

Rivera has painted the contemporary capitalist crisis in all its grotesque contradiction: idle machines needing workers, idle workers needing machines and the products of machines; choking granaries bursting with grain and hungering humans starving for a piece of bread; empty habitations that cannot find occupants while homeless workers sleep in parks and doorways, under bridges, in cellars and in vacant lots; careworn, ragged, freezing breadlines, subsisting on old crusts and "slop" while the Brazilian government pays the plantation owners to burn millions of bags of coffee and the American government pays the farmers to burn millions of tons of wheat.

THE BONUS MARCH

Washington is used to lobbyists. They come in droves. They arrive in Pullmans, put up at the best hotels and mansions; buttonhole Congressmen in exclusive clubs, present vast and vague expense accounts, and secure the legislation they have come to get. But lobbyists in working clothes, lobbyists in torn remnants of army "O. D.'s," lobbyists in overalls, arriving on freight trains or on foot, lobbyists with no manners and no expense accounts, no letters of introduction and no "contingent funds," no Washington address and often no home address, lobbyists in masses and the masses appearing in their own behalf as lobbyists, to demand from the "people's representatives" that on this issue they should represent the people—this spectacle put terror into the hearts of official Washington.

Secretary of War Hurley, Major General Douglas McArthur, General Pelham D. Glassford, Superintendent of the Washington Police, the Burns Agency, the secret service, the marines, the capitol police, the military police, and the army of the United States with full equipment of machine guns, rifles, bayonets, hand grenades, gas bombs and tanks, were mobilized for the famous Battle of Anacostia Flats. Were ever veterans of a foreign war given a warmer reception by the officials of a grateful nation?

The strategy of Generals Glassford and McArthur contained elements of contradiction: on the one hand to brand as "Communist" the whole expedition of 20,000 unemployed veterans, many with wives and children accompanying them from the four corners of America, and on the other to separate the small contingent of actual communists and their sympathizers from the mass of "loyal," i.e., illusion-burdened veterans.

A furious press campaign, demagogic scheming by Glassford, the work of stool-pigeons and Burns agents whom the government maneuvered into the leadership of the Bonus Expeditionary Force, rough-house tactics by government agents in the B. E. F. against every sign of militancy, certain tactical blunders by the Communists, and the natural rawness of the men, all combined to effect the first objective of the government—the isolation of the illusion-burdened mass from

STOP
FARMERS HOLIDAY
HUNGER MARCH

the Bonus [illegible]
sion of the [illegible] for the [illegible]
government which [illegible]
through the [illegible]
bonus to the [illegible]
daily. The "people's [illegible]
of the night while the [illegible]
were assuring them [illegible]
veterans did not [illegible]
picketing the White [illegible]
Five days after Congress [illegible]
of Columbia ordered the [illegible]
army of citizens [illegible]

The army attacked with [illegible]
supported by machine [illegible]
trained for it in their [illegible]
gas are no respecter of [illegible]
children were less hardy [illegible]
the long trek "home." [illegible]
L. Tauber Davison and Secretary [illegible]
"baby killer" when they [illegible]
"loyal" of bodies, the American [illegible]
ment of the attack [illegible]
of the great crisis which Loyalty [illegible]

[illegible]

Whole milk with all the cream [illegible]
skimmed milk, grades A, B and C [illegible]
the city dweller! [illegible] centers of [illegible]
members of the Chamber of Commerce [illegible]
pelt each other with their [illegible]
fuel in the Middle West [illegible]

the "Reds." But in proportion as the first aim was attained, the illusions of the rank and file of the veterans were dissipated; for the government which was handing out billions to the railways and banks through the R. F. C. did not intend to lend a penny of their future bonus to the jobless ex-soldiers. The militancy of the B. E. F. mounted daily. The "people's representatives." adjourned secretly in the dead of the night while the government agents in the ranks of the marchers were assuring them that Congress would not adjourn. Still the veterans did not go home—they had no homes to go to! They began picketing the White House to demand a special session of Congress. Five days after Congress adjourned, the Commissioners of the District of Columbia ordered the evacuation of Washington by the "invading army" of citizens. Two veterans were killed by Glassford's police.

The army attacked with fixed bayonets, gas bombs, flaming torches supported by machine gun squads and tanks. The veterans had been trained for it in their service to "their country," yet tear and mustard gas are no respecter of "trained" lungs and eyes. The women and children were less hardy and several babies died a few days later on the long trek "home." Months afterward, Assistant Secretary of War, F. Trubee Davison, and Secretary Hurley, were greeted with cries of "baby-killer" when they tried to address conventions of that most "loyal" of bodies, the American Legion. Rivera has painted the moment of the attack, with the camp in flames, as a memorable aspect of the great crisis which began in 1929.

THE FARMERS' HOLIDAY

Whole milk with all the cream at 2 cents a quart to the farmer; skimmed milk, grades A, B and C at 10, 12, 14 and 16 cents a quart to the city dweller! At Petaluma, center of the white leghorn industry, members of the Chamber of Commerce dress in medieval armor and pelt each other with fresh laid eggs by the case full. Grain used as fuel in the Middle West; cotton and cabbages plowed under in Louisiana; watermelons bobbing up and down along the Suwanee River; peaches selling at 5 cents a piece in New York and Chicago; peaches rotting under the Georgia trees because the farmer cannot get back the expense of crating and shipping them when he sells them to the produce companies; farm prices fallen to 60% of the pre-war levels, but farmers paying 266% of their pre-war taxes; the farm dollar shrinking faster than the city dollar and, when inflation comes, the city dollar swelling like a balloon before the farm dollar reaches the proportions of a soap bubble; bankers' mortgages shrinking not a penny while the land the mortgage money bought is shrinking 30% to 50% in value; forced sales and voluntary and involuntary bankruptcies affecting one-quarter of all the farms in America; 40,000 farms sold up for taxes at a single tax sale in Mississippi; farm families homeless, wandering up and down the highways of the land, riding the freights, filling the tin-can jungles, vainly working the skidways; farmers driven into the workless working-class and listening bewildered, embittered, to speeches in praise of the joys of country life; farmers bribed and coerced by the government into the criminal activity of burning their wheat fields, plowing in the crops on which they have labored, withdrawing their land from cultivation.

The center of the panel shows starving unemployed plunging their fingers into a garbage can in search of edible refuse, while behind them can be seen farmers pouring milk into the creek, mountains of fruit and vegetables rotting in the fields, farmers setting fire to the waving acres of precious wheat.

The years 1932 and 1933 saw big farmers' revolts, milk strikes, wheat strikes, mass resistance to foreclosure sales. The farmer who feeds America, the farmer whom facile journalistic analysts fancy to be the bulwark of conservatism, is in revolt. The milk-pouring portrayed on the left is being done by striking farmers, not to raise the price of milk in the cities but to raise their share of the price that is too high already.

On the right a sheriff is vainly trying to auction off a farm in a foreclosure sale while grim-faced determined farmers with taut muscles and narrowed eyes gather around to see that there is no bidding. Over the embarrassed representative of the law (and the mortgage company) hangs a threatening noose, and under his nose a solitary farmer delegated by his comrades is bidding a single dollar for the farm. There will be no other bids! For a dollar it will sell, and then go back mortgage-free to its original owner. The scenes from Shays' Rebellion from the opposing panel on the other wall are repeating themselves. Humble Americans are living up to their revolutionary traditions.

In the foreground, in a scene of tremendous power and movement, reminiscent in its composition of the stirring sketches by Albrecht Dürer of the peasants' wars, are being re-enacted other scenes from Shays' Rebellion—but the country's troops are better armed with gas bombs and helmets and masks, while the revolting American farmers are no longer armed as were Shays' men in a freer day; they have improvised their arms from the wood pile and axle tree.

In the central triangle, broken derelicts sleep on the stone steps of the sub-treasury bursting with stocks of gold; below are the hungry harvesters of garbage. But in all the portrayal of misery, there is a note of hope, for the spirit of resistance is not dead.

Hunger marchers, bonus marchers, foreclosure fighters, farm strikers, starvation in the midst of plenty, and the army of the United States and National Guard to see that the hungry do not get their food, that the veterans do not get their bonus, that the farmers do not get the cost of production nor save their farms from foreclosure—such is Rivera's living, stirring picture of the depression.

THE "New Deal" was a brilliantly conceived slogan. The despair surrounding the Hoover administration with its steadily sinking economy, its deadlocked congressional line-up, and its mounting misery, was an excellent preparation for a mood of new illusions and fresh hopes. The Hoover administration was paralyzed by an approaching election, by a deadlocked Congress, by a heavy heritage of Harding-Coolidge-Hoover traditional policy, by a singular ineptitude for that prime requisite of modern statesmanship, demagogy. But the Roosevelt era began with a new administration, a great political "change" (from "Republicanism" to "Democracy") a huge Congressional majority, a frightened and bewildered people who had already abandoned their golden calf and were crying aloud for a Moses to lead his sheep out of the wilderness and into the promised land.

NEW DEAL STRATEGY

The essence of the "New Deal," peculiarly enough, is identical with the essence of the Hoover program. Hoover dreamed of setting aside the anti-trust laws and permitting price-fixing and the completion of the trustification of American industry; Roosevelt has made the dream a reality. Hoover cut the wages of the federal employees; Roosevelt extended the cut. Hoover vetoed the bonus bill, using gas and flame and bayonet to disperse the bonus-marchers. Roosevelt sent his wife instead of the military to greet the second bonus march, provided army tents and "mulligan" instead of gas bombs, but vetoed the bonus bill again and did what Hoover had not dared to do, cut the veteran disability allowances by $400,000,000. In the course of a year, Hoover gave over two billions in subsidies and loans to banks and corporations through the Reconstruction Finance Corporation. In his first three months in office Roosevelt advanced a larger amount than Hoover had in an entire year.

Hamstrung by a hostile Congress, Hoover dreamt of an executive dictatorship; Roosevelt induced a friendly congress to vote away its powers to him in the fields of industry, agriculture, tariff, budget, currency, and banking. Hoover's proposals for increasing the navy were greeted with denunciation; Roosevelt laid down a program of 102 new ships and 2,000 airplanes without a murmur of congressional opposition. Hoover had the unhappy gift of making every measure appear as an affront to the mass of the American people, a seven-league stride in reaction, whereas Roosevelt has a genius for making the realization of the same proposal appear as a favor to the masses, a mile post on the march of progress.

The main features of Roosevelt generalship are:

1. Act quickly, act often—something new every minute;

2. Dramatize every action—everything large or small must be heralded, proclaimed with trumpet blast, "sold" to the public;

3. Take the public into the "secret"—it is not necessary to explain everything about any measure but it is necessary to explain something about every measure;

4. Keep the initiative—no matter what happens as the result of the depression it must appear that it was done purposely—banks are closing in state after state, close them all and hail the depression disaster as a triumph of statesmanship, as a biblical scourging of the money changers from God's temple. America has had wholesale bank closings and bank "holidays" before, America and other nations have previously been forced off the gold standard by economic crisis, but it took an especial gift for statecraft to make these disasters appear as deliberate strokes of genius to combat the depression.

5. Concentration of power in the hands of the chief executive, entrust things to the "leader"—he will lead us to the new promised land.

The central conception of Rivera's "New Deal" panel is contained in the playful portrait of the little blue eagle in the big brown shirt that occupies the central foreground of the panel. His estimate of the NRA is expressed in the slogan: *"Workers Unite! Or the blue eagle will wear a brown shirt. NRA paves the way for fascism."*

Like fascism, the NRA concentrates a tremendous amount of economic power in the hands of the "leader." There is a similar increase in the closeness of union between government and business, a similar expediting of trustification and state capitalism, a similar trend to economic nationalism, acceleration of military preparedness. Like fascism, the "New Deal" surrounds the realization of the program of big business with a halo of social demagogy.

But the analogy should not be pushed too far. American capitalism is too powerful; the labor movement too weak, too disorganized, too lacking in militancy and consciousness, for labor to be a serious contender for power. The employing class may and does infringe ruthlessly on civil liberties, but it finds no need to abolish them. The president may concentrate the essential powers of governmental economic policy in his hands, but he does it with the consent of Congress and the two major parties, and has no need of abolishing elections or parliamentarism. Above all, American capitalism is not so threatened by its working class that it needs to outlaw the unions and political organizations of the workers. Therefore Rivera's banner is an admonition to the workers, not an assertion of identity.

LABOR UNDER THE NEW DEAL

The NRA was supposed to effect re-employment by shortening the work week; stimulate production by raising prices and increasing the purchasing power of labor. But the work-week established by code in most industries was not shorter, but longer than the number of hours actually being worked by labor during the depression years. The wage

NRA
WE DO OUR PART
STRIKE.
STRIKE!
NRA
WORKERS UNITE!
Or the blue eagle WILL
wear a Brown shirt.
NRA PAVES THE WAY
FOR FASCISM!!

codes did little more than stabilize the sub-starvation wage levels of the depression, raising the lowest paid workers here and there, and leveling off the wages of the better paid. The only substantial re-employment provided during the first year of the NRA was in the militarized relief camps of the Civilian Conservation Corps and such "made work" relief ventures as the CWA. The inflationary rise in prices actually reduced the meager purchasing power of labor.

"COLLECTIVE BARGAINING"

While the NRA conceded to labor official right to organize, its operation automatically organized the employers on a nation-wide scale. Labor's "right" has been qualified by official interpretation, so that company "unions" are a legal expression of "collective bargaining." The strengthened employing class in the steel, auto, and other basic industries has flatly refused to permit unionization, and many employers, like Ford, have even rejected company unionism! At the same time, labor is menaced by the elevation of class collaboration into a fundamental governmental policy and the assumption by the state of the power to control hours and wages and interfere in the inner concerns of labor organizations.

Nevertheless, the NRA in more ways than one, has created a situation full of vantage points for the labor movement—vantage points no less real because unintended by the sponsors of the "New Deal."

With the initiation of the National Recovery Act in the fourth year of the profoundest depression in the history of American capitalism, the labor movement entered into a new period of development. The influence of the faint beginnings of upturn was reinforced by the widespread discussion of wages and hours, by the necessity of being represented in the formulation of the labor provisions of codes, by the illusions created by "New Deal" demagogy, by the widespread belief that unions and strikes had suddenly become "legal," "respectable," "backed by the government." The pent up resentment of four bitter years of wage cuts and employing class arrogance suddenly broke through. A great wave of strikes and struggles swept over the country. There was an influx of fresh blood into the enfeebled trade unions; the ideas of unionism and organization permeated hitherto untouched strata of the American working class. Hundreds of thousands of workers poured into the American Federation of Labor, raising its membership to the record high point of 1918-1919. A new spirit of self-confidence and militancy inspired the trade union membership, and even forced the moth-eaten conservative leadership to pay reluctant and startled tribute in unaccustomed language. Labor, after five years of apathy and stagnation under an ill-distributed "prosperity" and four years of helpless retreat under the blows of the depression, had begun to fight back.

This is the aspect of the "New Deal" which interests Rivera most and he has produced a dynamic panel full of strike struggle and conflict. In the background gunmen, detectives, and police are seeking to stem the rising tide of militancy with the time-honored weapons of armed force. The scenes are derivative from the fierce struggles of the coal miners in the "captive mines" owned by the steel companies. In the center are a mass of needle trades pickets being sentenced wholesale for violating an injunction against picketing a shop which bore the blue eagle and the legend "We do our part."

The model for the gentle judge is derived from the imposing figure of Judge Ewald, whom the Seabury commission charged with paying $10,000 for his magistracy.

In the foreground are scenes from the struggles of the dressmakers on the picket line, who, militantly and capably led, struck to dictate the code for their industry, with excellent results. Rivera has put this struggle in the foreground to suggest what possibilities there are for progressive unionism to take advantage of the new labor situation created by the "New Deal."

PANEL XVI DIVISION AND DEPRESSION

A LONG breadline that stretches out to the horizon shows the present plight of the jobless workers. The rest of the panel is given over to a huge unemployment demonstration—a demonstration big enough to suggest the possibility of putting an end to the spectacle of breadlines in the richest country in the world—were it not for the divisions in the working class. The signs of those divisions occupy the foreground of the picture.

Two mounted police are riding into the demonstration—just on the point of provocative attack. One of them has his club raised, his

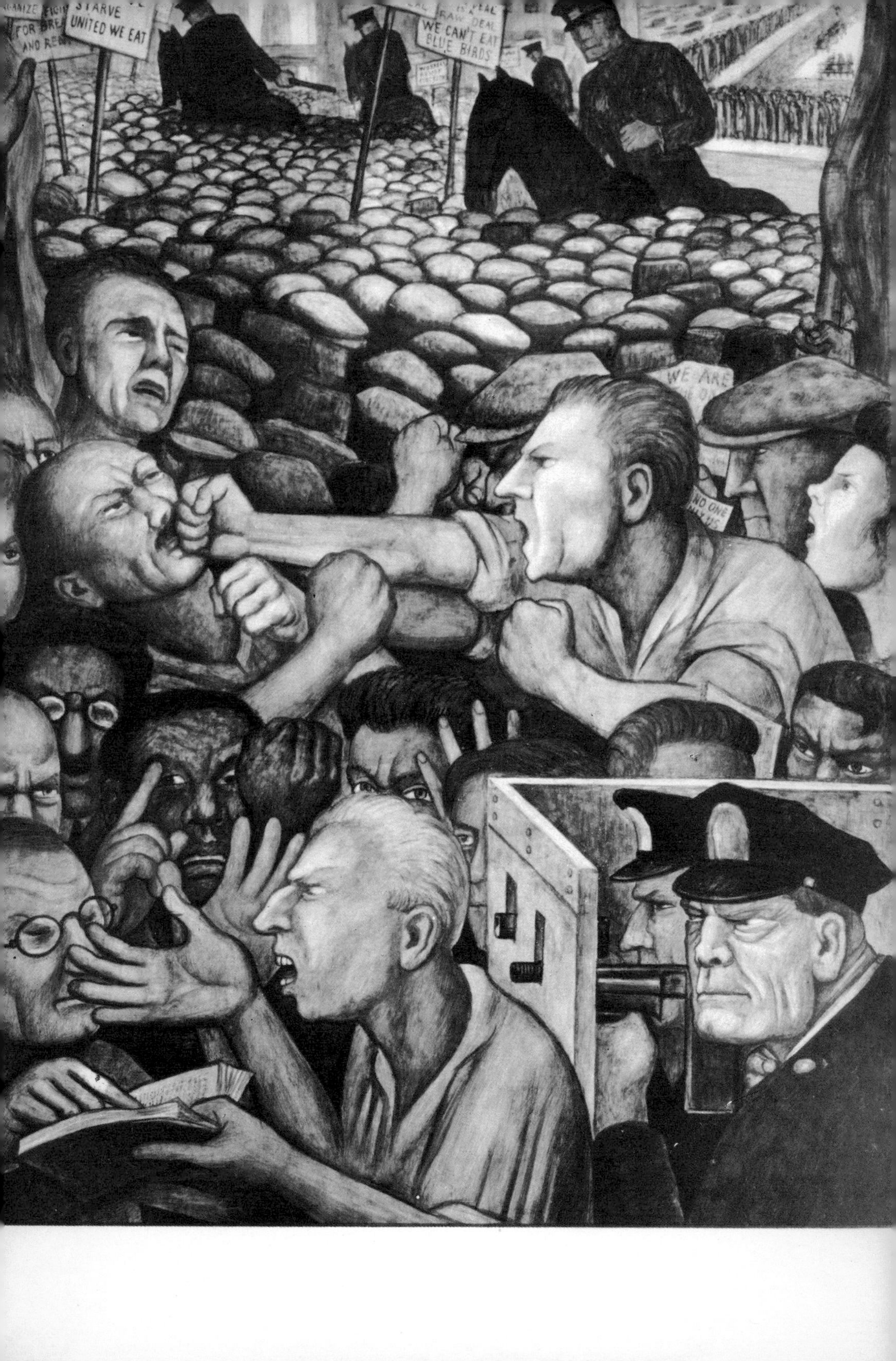

STARVE
UNITED WE EAT
RAW DEAL
WE CAN'T EAT
BLUE BIRDS
WE ARE
NO ONE

arm about to swing. In another moment it will crack a head. In another moment the deep-flowing quiet river of sluggish resentment will be a raging, flying torrent of imprecations and screams of workers fleeing and workers fighting back, of shrieking sirens and police whistles, barking armored motorcycles, and perhaps machine guns. The spectator holds his breath and watches for the "riot" to begin. This demonstration of the unemployed is a reproduction of a portion of the destroyed mural at Rockefeller Center.

The great central mass of the demonstration, representing the mass of the unemployed workers, is compact and solid. Over it rise signs calling for proletarian unity: "Unemployed Organize"; "Divided We Starve—United We Eat." But as we approach the foreground, fragments of signs show a different spirit: "We are the Only . . ."; "No One . . . Only Us." Here there is no solidarity, no unity. Here are strident voices in violent altercation, no one listening to the other, all striving to be heard. Here are the exalted passions of worker quarreling with worker, of doctrinaire debating with doctrinaire. Discussion has become vituperation and vituperation has begun to yield to exchange of blows. A leader of the demonstration with raised hand is vainly trying to quiet the tumult. Two workers in the foreground have converted a Communist book into a Talmudic text and are with complacent excitement drawing opposite conclusions from the same passage, while one of them, in the enthusiasm of his exposition, has unwittingly backed up against an armored machine gun shield behind which grim-faced police are preparing to "let 'em have it" the moment the "riot" begins.

The foreground is eloquent with restless flying hands, expressive hands reminiscent of those of the opposing panel (Panel I) facing this picture on the other wall. It is the hands, more than anything else, that give the feeling of disquiet to the picture; a feeling that is emphasized when the mural is seen *in situ* by the fact that the visual supports for the ceiling that Rivera has painted into all the other panels are here dim and inadequate. The buildings in the background are too obscured to give the sensation of supports, and cardboard signs and cloth banners and an upstretched hand that seems to strive in vain to support its visual burden, are poor props indeed and add to the uneasy feeling of confusion and disorder that pervades this picture of working class division in the face of mass misery, brutal attack, and the burning need for unity.

Out of the world war and the break in the capitalist system, out of the crisis and the inability of capitalism to extricate itself by the old procedures, out of the divisions in the working class and their inability to organize the proletarian way out of the crisis—out of these antecedents has come fascism. Therefore, Rivera has painted this scene of working class disunity as the last picture on this side rather than next to the depression panel, because the divisions in the ranks of the Communist Party, the coalition with bourgeois parties on the part of the Socialists, the putting of sect, clique, or faction interests above the elementary interest of the working class in its own unity, have paved the way for the victories of Italian and German fascism portrayed on the rear wall.

PANELS XVII & XVIII MUSSOLINI AND HITLER

IN the countries where the working class is within striking distance of power, the bourgeoisie is no longer able to rule in the old way, and reluctantly calls in the banditti of naked force to rule in its behalf. It sacrifices its decaying political system that it may retain a little longer the economic power that has become incompatible with the further development of the forces of production. Not that it has not used force as occasion required throughout its history, but now force is not occasional but permanent, not last resort but first instance, not concealed but naked—force raised to the level of an official system.

The bourgeoisie shrinks backward because it dare not push forward. Confidence in the future—the dogma of progress—gives place to frightened recourse to the poetry of the past—to Roman legions, pagan nature gods, consular fasces, Aryan swastikas, the headsman's axe, the ancient inquisitorial infamies. Such are the ingredients of which fascism is compounded—the elements out of which Rivera has built his Mussolini and Hitler panels.

The two fascist panels form a single structural unit in rhythm and composition. Mussolini is balanced by Hitler; the tricolor with axe and fasces by the red swastika banner; the foreground masses are constructed of supporters and victims of the two regimes; the inner side of each picture culminates in a line of marching, steel-helmeted, gas-masked men, surmounted by planes—armed forces from both fascist lands marching to the attack on the Soviet Union.

As the rhythms of the Nazi panel repeat those of the Fascist, so the broad outlines of the rise to power of Hitler in Germany repeat those of Mussolini's rise in Italy. Essentially, the two movements represent the same content—the same superheated nationalism, the same preliminary support by a desperate, ruined, uprooted middle class, disillusioned by working class failure to break through to victory; the same recruiting of the declassed offscourings of the *lumpenproletariat* and even of large sections of the workers, especially the youth and permanently unemployed; the same emotionalism and bombast; the same glorification of violence both in domestic and international affairs; the same sadistic brutality and cruelty; the same tendency on the part of the ruined middle class, which has lost confidence in its own powers, to place all hope in "il Duce," "der Fuehrer," a leader-saviour-superman, who is to lead them out of a hopeless situation; the same skillful demagogy, the non-essentials and external trappings of social revolution, to harness these despairing classes and sections of classes to the program of great capital.

THE NATIONAL IMPRESS

But just as the bourgeois republic differs in France and America, just as capitalism itself shows infinite variations and gradations in appearance due to natural environment, racial peculiarities, traditional and historical influences from land to land, so these essentially identical movements bear upon them the impress of their respective countries of origin, differences which reflect themselves clearly in Rivera's portrayal.

Italian fascism borrows its memories from ancient Rome. Its symbol, the fasces, was carried before the Roman consuls to signify their power to punish (the rods) and their power over life and death (the axe). The eagle surmounting the Italian tri-color is the emblem of the Roman legions. Roman, too, are the salute and the battle cry; the consuls, cohorts, centuries, maniples, legions; the quadrivirate that directed the march on Rome; the Caesarism of *il Duce* and the dream of lordship over the Mediterranean world.

The black shirt is Italian, a memory of Garibaldi's red-shirt march on Rome; and Hitler's brown shirts and the blue, green, silver and all the other shirts of other lands are merely an evidence of unoriginality, and echoes of the khaki uniforms of the world war.

The elements of theatricality and mock-heroics in Italian political life are suggested in the fixed frown and studied pose of Mussolini, the battery of cameras and microphones, the statue of *il Duce* with one foot planted on top of the world.

The torture scenes of the background have a distinctive stamp. Italian fascism rode to power with canes, stilettos, revolvers, bombs, gasoline, castor oil, plumed and helmeted *arditi,* punitive expeditions of cavalry or motor trucks shooting indiscriminately and setting fire to cooperatives, *casas dal popolo,* newspapers, and communal halls in towns with Socialist or Communist majorities. In the upper left the famous castor oil "discipline" is being visited at the point of a stiletto; clubs and lashes are in play; gasoline has been applied to set a *camera dal lavoro,* a union headquarters, in flames; a firing squad with comparative mercy is making short shrift of some rebel workers.

A striking difference between the German and the Italian panel lies in the presence of German figures exclusively (despite Hitler we must include the Jews!) in the former, and the presence of various non-Italian figures in the latter. In part this is due to the collocation of the Mussolini panel near the "New Deal" picture on the side wall: the presence of the admiring university professor, the lady of "high society," Father Cox, the commander of the American Legion and the hooded figure of the Klansman, is Rivera's way of indicating the elements of fascism in American life. But there are other "alien" figures. J. P. Morgan, in the foreground, and behind Mussolini the grim figure of John Bull with many bank notes in his hand. There are no such figures in the Hitler panel. Italy aspires to empire, but it is no first-rate power. It lacks coal, it lacks iron, it lacks oil, it lacks accumulated capital reserves. In any game for world empire, for all Mussolini's rhetoric, it can play but the role of a junior partner to Anglo-American imperialism.

But Germany is no pawn in the game of nations. The Dawes Plan days are over. German capitalism is arming, goose-stepping, uniforming its whole people, in a mad attempt to become again in its own right a first-rate imperialist power.

THE BLESSING OF THE POPE

Behind Mussolini stands the Pope administering the papal blessing. Early fascism was demagogically anti-monarchical and anti-clerical. But Mussolini's advent to power was by His Majesty's order, and he renounced his republicanism in a sycophantic speech, for he found the monarchy useful in legalizing his coup and in giving a sense of conservative stability to the fascist "revolution." His conflict with the Vatican was more serious, for it too aspired to be the ruler of Italy, and there was some conflict between the big landowners and the industrialists as to the nature of the "new" Italy. Moreover, the church was unfavorable to fascism's claim to control all mass organizations. But after the black shirts had smashed the "Popular" party, the Catholic trade unions and municipal administrations along with the Socialist and Communist, the Concordat was signed and the trinity of reaction, Pope, King and Duce, was arrived at on the condition that the three should be one, and that one—Mussolini.

BENITO MUSSOLINI

The two panels center in the figures of their respective "leaders." Mussolini is the greater actor; Hitler the more violent demagogue and agitator. Over Mussolini hovers the shadow of Caesar and Bonaparte; Hitler echoes Bismarck and . . . Siegfried! Mussolini shows the traces of his pre-war "left" socialism—in reality a dilution of socialism with Italian syndicalism, a philosophical glorification of violence for its own sake after the fashion of Sorel. It was this syndicalist "leftism" that raised Mussolini, a young school teacher, to the editorship of the Socialist organ *Avanti* at the age of 25. It was this worship of violence on an international scale that won him expulsion from the party in

A.L

1914 as pro-war. Pro-Allied industrialists began financing Mussolini's paper and organization which went from war agitation to strike-breaking, and from strike-breaking to smashing of unions, cooperatives, and agrarian leagues, and thence to the present seat of power.

There is much that is specifically Prussian in Hitler's technique. There is the playing of soldier, the military spirit that has been bred into the German people for several decades: the heel-clicking, the salutes, the uniforms, the furious drumming, the trumpet blasts, the elaborately staged parades, the handing out of titles, the exaction of absolute obedience, the concentration of power in the commander-in-chief. Hitler studied Italian fascism, learned lessons from its technique, but carefully Germanized it in every detail. If Mussolini's fascism shows the stamp of its Italian syndicalist origin, Hitler's National Socialism bears the mark of its birth in a milieu of a Social-Democratic and Communist working class. The Nazis borrowed "Socialist" for the title of their party. They borrowed all the Communist criticisms of the inaction and compromise and corruption of the Social-Democratic officials who had ruled Germany. They took advantage of the Communist weakness of talking too much of Moscow and not enough of the problems of the German masses, to brand the German Communists as "hired Moscow agents." But they borrowed freely from Communism —its red banners, its battle cries, its slogans, its songs, all the externalities with none of the class content of its agitation and propaganda— "red songs with black words."

NAZI KULTUR

"It was the 'prestige of violence,'" declared Mussolini, "that gave victory to the Fascist candidates. The great popular mass submitted to the fascination of violence, which is the creator and resuscitator of enthusiasms."

But German Nazism improved upon the methods of "fascinating" the masses—less poetry eulogizing violence, more thoroughness and superior scientific technique in its application.

Rivera has built his Hitler picture around the words "Nazi Kultur." In the foreground (left) is Professor Einstein, living symbol of the systematic man-hunt to drive every thinker, every scholar, every active and critical mind out of German University life.

Next to Einstein is the tortured body of a Jew, whose sin is in his "blood." The demagogy which sought to short-circuit the anti-capitalist resentment of the German masses by turning it into the channel of a campaign against "international Jewish capital" and "international Jewish Marxism" nevertheless gives careful protection to the Jewish stockbroker, the Jewish banker, the Jewish department-store owner, while it lets loose a raging fury against the Jewish professional man, the Jewish civil servant, scientist, or artist.

Next to the portrait of the Jew is the Christian girl who has endangered the "purity" of the "Aryan" race and is doing penance by being paraded through the streets with shaven head and lacerated flesh bearing the sign "I have given myself to a Jew." The face of the storm-trooper reveals that here as in the case of positions what has been taken from the Jew will fall into "nobler and purer" hands.

Symbol of Nazi Kultur is the bloodthirsty Goering (to the right of the tortured girl) raised from a dope-addict's cell in an insane asylum to the right hand of "the leader." The top ranks of this movement of "redemption" swarm with common criminals who have prison records for burglary, arson, counterfeiting, forgery, manslaughter, white-slavery and homosexual prostitution.

Symbol of Nazi Kulture is the sterilization operation portrayed in the center of the panel—modern science put at the service of barbaric terror. Nazi Kultur manifests itself in the "night of the long knives" of which Strasser boasted, while the long knife hovers over the heads of Thaelman (above Einstein), Törgler, and Brandler, leaders of the German Communist movement.

It is manifest in the revival of the medieval headsman whose

NAZI KULTUR
I HAVE GIVEN
MYSELF TO A JEW

function is a gala affair to be performed in formal dress in fulfillment of the prophecy of the Leader—"heads will roll when we come into power." Here is one promise that was redeemed in ample fashion.

It is manifest in the systematic crushing of opponents through hunger, cold, sickness, moral degradation, bestial indignities, sadistic tortures, in the detention camps pictured in the background—in blows from rubber clubs, from wet sandbags that tear the kidneys, the holding of wives and children and aged parents as hostages, the reintroduction of torture as an authorized method of extracting information, the death penalty for circulating underground literature, the jailing of hundreds of thousands, the 3,000 officially reported cases of those "shot trying to escape" or meeting death in concentration camps through "accident" or "suicide."

And Nazi Kultur is lighting the "night of the long knives" with the bright flames of the fires in which are consumed, so far as fire can consume, all that is worth while in German literature, philosophy, art, and science. The flames that rise from the works of Remarque and Mann and Thalheimer, Boas, Trotsky, and Einstein, Lenin, Engels, and Marx, and countless other treasures of the human spirit, curve over towards the panel representing social progress, the next step in human development, Socialism. The curve is paralleled in the hands raised in fascist salute, strangely like projectiles beginning their flight, in the helmeted, gas-masked, bayoneted, marching armies, in the tanks and airplanes—flames, projectiles, tanks, armies, planes, all moving in the direction of the central panel representing the Soviet Union.

THIS central panel gives the impression of a solid foundation, monumental blocks hewn out of granite—the eye finds repose after the restless, agitated movement of the strike panel, the panel of proletarian disunity, the fascist panels of barbaric cruelty and torture.

The picture is dominated by the imposing figure of Lenin, joining the hands of an American white worker and an American Negro worker, the hands of a soldier and the hands of a farmer, in fraternal union. It is a reproduction of the Lenin theme in Radio City.

Lenin is flanked by the figures of Marx and Engels. At the shoulders of Lenin are Rosa Luxemburg (left) and Clara Zetkin (right), the two outstanding woman leaders that the international working class has produced.

To the left of Marx is Stalin, and below him Bukharin, to the right of Engels the figure of Leon Trotsky. Stalin, Bukharin, and Trotsky represented three tendencies in the Communist movement of the Soviet Union, a division which led to dissension and split.

In the left foreground are the figures of William Z. Foster, Chairman of the American Communist Party (official or Stalinist group), Jay Lovestone, Secretary of the Communist Party of the United States (Opposition), and James P. Cannon, Secretary of the American Trotskyites. The placing of these three figures together is the painter's plea for American Communist unity.

On the lower right are Charles E. Ruthenberg, till his death outstanding organizer and leader of the American Party, and Bertram D. Wolfe.

Again recur the eloquent hands characteristic of Rivera's portraiture: the eager, nervous, taut hand of the teacher, seeking to point out to the American workers the Leninist path to Communist unity

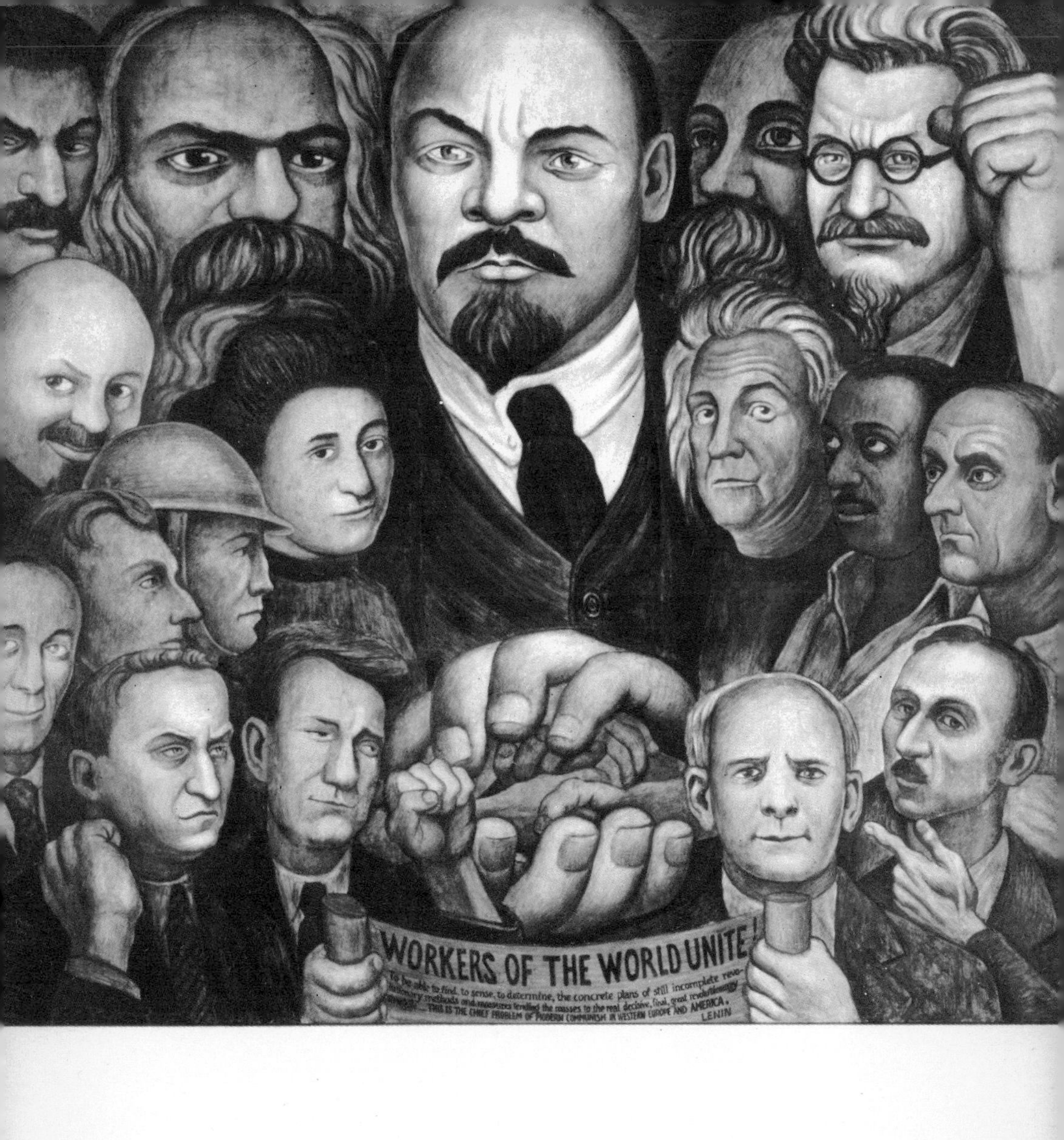
WORKERS OF THE WORLD UNITE!
To be able to find, to sense, to determine, the concrete plans of still incomplete revo-
THIS IS THE CHIEF PROBLEM OF MODERN COMMUNISM IN WESTERN EUROPE AND AMERICA.
LENIN

and working class solidarity and power; the clenched fists of the fighters in the cause of communism, the powerful, all-embracing hands of Lenin, firmly joining together the hands of black worker and white, of workers with soldier and farmer, in a common union of all the oppressed against the rising tide of fascism and rebarbarization, of crisis and war, in a common struggle for a workers' world.

Between the two portrayals of fascism and the Lenin panel are two smaller painted spaces over the two doors that flank the central section. These small panels represent the forces of resistance against fascism and defense of the workers' land.

Over the right door, adjoining the Hitler panel, a young worker with powerful, flexed arm holds back a hand wielding a blood-stained fascist dagger marked with a swastika. Behind the young worker is a red flag with hammer and sickle (page 232).

Over the left door, facing the Mussolini panel, a young Negro and an elderly white workingman are choking an eagle and breaking the fasces, the bundle of sticks symbolic of Mussolini's power. The eagle has a double intention—it is the eagle of "Roman" fascism, but the bird is painted blue! (see page 232).

The two small panels together are another expression of the painter's urgent plea for the unity of white worker and black, of young worker and old, against the rising wave of fascist barbarism.

It is with this plea that Rivera ends his work. On the two long side walls he has portrayed the moving story of the development of America from the colonial period up to the days of the NRA. He has traced the life cycle of the birth, growth, and maturity of American capitalism, and, in the later panels, the multiplying signs of its decay.

Throughout the series have run two opposing forces in conflict. The one of them expresses the "negative" side of American life: extermination of the Indians, enslavement of the Negroes, exploitation of the workers, the tradition of the lash, the chain-gang, the use of troops against strikers, lynch law, the frame up, the Ku Klux Klan.

This tendency culminates in the fascist panels on the rear wall.

The other expresses the progressive aspect of American development: the war for independence, the struggle for the abolition of slavery, the generous vision of the transcendentalists, the creative power of the inventors and scientists, the productivity of American industry, the struggles of American labor. This tendency culminates in proletarian unity and the victory of the new social order—the central panel of the rear wall.

Once again, as at the birth of America, two social systems exist side by side. Amid the death agonies of feudalism and the birth pangs of capitalism America was discovered, explored, settled. Amid the death agonies of capitalism and the birth pangs of socialism, America has attained to a stormy and contested hegemony which links it up inseparably with the rest of the world.

The rear wall is thus taken up by the opposing forces of reaction and further progress. The outcome of the struggle between them will determine the fate of America as of all mankind.